ENERGETIC SELLING AND MARKETING

ENERGETIC SELLING AND MARKETING

*A new way to create extraordinary growth
in your business*

by

LENKA LUTONSKA

*The practical and spiritual guide
for purpose-driven women in business*

'No matter how far you have come,
there is more to your business potential
than you can ever imagine.'

Edited by Wendy Yorke
Published by Shimran
an imprint of Fitzrovia Press
Glastonbury BA6 8HF, UK

www.fitzroviapress.co.uk

ISBN 978-0-9570722-5-1

printed and bound in Great Britain
by
Grosvenor Group Print Services Ltd
Essex IG10 3TS
text on FSC bookwove 80gsm
cover on 300gsm 2 Sided Board

DEDICATION

To every woman with a calling in her heart:

'You are meant for something bigger'

Acknowledgements

My heartfelt thanks to all those people who have helped me to become who I am today, and to write, edit and publish my book.

My husband Tomas: the love of my life and my rock; without your unwavering support I would not be able to do what I do.

My incredible clients, from all over the world; the source of my inspiration and support while I was writing this book and their successes, which validate the Energetic Selling and Marketing Principles.

Tatiana, Lorna, Amy, Debbie and all my business team, who have provided me with heaps of accountability, inspiration and advice.

My coaches and mentors, who have helped me on my business journey.

Wendy Yorke: my book coach and literary editor; without her belief in my ideas and second-to-none support throughout the process, this book would still only be an idea in my mind.

Ranchor Prime: my publisher and the founder of Fitzrovia Press.

And lastly, thank you my dear reader; I could not have done it without you.

FOREWORD

BY PENNY POWER OBE

I speak at a huge number of conferences and I experience a vast array of speaking styles and hear so much knowledge being shared. It is hard to stand out in this crowded market. However, when I heard Lenka Lutonska present at the 2018 Female Speakers Conference, I was totally blown away.

Lenka was billed as a lady who was going to speak about selling. A subject I know well because I have always been a sales person trained professionally and attended many courses when I was leading a team of 300 sales people in the 1980s and 90s. I sat back in my seat and hoped to enjoy Lenka's approach to business and life, and the important part which sales plays.

However, more than enjoy, I was wonderfully energised and motivated by Lenka's talk because I realised that I had forgotten many aspects. I was soon sitting bolt upright and writing many notes to myself. For this reason, it is such a joy and a privilege to write the Forward for her fabulous first book.

Life is changing fast and we need to tap into these changes to thrive. People who say 'business has always been the same' are simply not connected, dare I say, 'they are the dinosaurs' and there are many of them. The connected world has created an energy, which when understood, can be very powerful to plug into. Lenka's ability to combine a new consciousness with her knowledge of business is brilliant.

We are all seeking the human side of life, including the ability to: trust; be a whole person; respect our whole being and that of other people; and to combine our sense of purpose with our business needs for income. Critically, to put the heart into our business life so we can be real for ourselves and for other people. Business needs to be taken seriously and we all want to succeed, to be a winner in our own definition of what that is. We want to reap rewards and to have an action-based mindset, as well as being purpose-driven.

I love Lenka's book and I hope everyone who reads it will experience the same tingle of inspiration that Lenka gave me when I first heard her speak. She continues to inspire me.

Penny Power OBE
Founder and CEO, The Business Cafe

PRAISE FOR THIS BOOK

'Lenka marries business growth strategies with powerful mindset and energy work in a way that I have never experienced before. Using her principles, I tripled my multiple-six figure business in six months and went over £1,000,000.'
Leigh Daniel, CEO Project Positive Change

'Energetic Selling is the new black. It is elegant, sexy, powerful, and will get you whatever you want in your business! It marries quantum physics and hot strategy and the result is dynamite! Proven and powerful, this book is world-class, results-proven, and provides a unified field of explosive business growth golden wisdom. A new quantum success paradigm is happening all around us and Lenka is proving that not only is she a pioneer, but she takes her students with her to mastery.'
Jenni Parker Brown, Founder Iconic Life Blueprint™ and the Trinity Code™

'Lenka's techniques are mind-blowing and her process has helped me understand how to use my energy in selling. In fact, these principles are 'world-shifting' and this book is a must read!'
Tania Dakka, Copywriter and creator of Copy Edge

'This book presents a totally new approach to business. It will revolutionise the world of selling and marketing.'
Tatiana Fecikova, Transformational Coach for Online Entrepreneurs

'Reading Lenka's book made everything click into place for me. Her writing is so approachable. Her back story and where she has come from made me realise that I was holding myself back from moving forward with my business and making excuses for not getting out there and winning my pitches.'
Lyndsey Ng, Publicist

'For so many of us on our entrepreneurial journey, money is the massive elephant in the room. We build our businesses around our passions and helping other people and then when it comes to selling and marketing ourselves, we simply get … stuck. There is a huge struggle in finding the balance between being of service to others and getting handsomely rewarded for our expertise. Lenka's book is an essential read for anyone that is desperately tried to align those parts of her business and actually fall in love with putting themselves out there, attracting their rockstar clients and earning lots of money. Like a modern day Marianne Williamson, she lovingly guides us through the simple, but incredibly powerful steps we can take to achieve extraordinary growth in our businesses. Her own story is inspirational enough, but this book is also packed with amazing stories of clients she has worked with who will have you beating a path to her door as soon as you have read the last page.'
Jessica Killingley, Marketing Consultant

'Having known Lenka for more than ten years I am delighted she has finally put all her advice, experiences and teachings

into one book. This is aimed a female coaches but with great advice for any entrepreneur who wants to create a profitable business while serving their ideal clients. Energetic Selling is a treasure trove of useful practical tools and ideas, illustrated with examples, of how you can successfully establish and grow your business. It makes you realise that the only limitations on success are related to your attitude and mindset. By implementing the advice in this book, changing your beliefs and working on your energy, you can have a very successful business. A must-read for anyone on their journey to becoming a successful entrepreneur.'
Debbie Gilbert, Founder of Mums Unlimited and author of
The Successful Mumpreneur

'What I love about Energetic Selling is how simple and yet how deep it actually is. It challenges the status quo of selling and marketing. Reading this book made me feel courageous. It made me feel like showing up for my vision doesn't have to be in any specific way but my own way. If you are looking to become an extraordinary woman and an entrepreneur without sacrificing who you are, without losing the spark in your eyes. This book is for you. If you have been looking for a new perspective that actually incorporates energy and not only tactics, I strongly recommend this book.'
Katya Varbanova, Video Marketing Strategist and creator of
20K Nation

'Admittedly, I'm not a woman. But I read this book non-stop cover-to-cover—and immediately started putting the principles into practice—and getting results!'
Gerry Maguire Thompson, bestselling author and #1 UK
expert in teaching standup comedy for business
communication skills

ABOUT THE AUTHOR

Lenka Lutonska was born in Slovakia and moved to the United Kingdom at the age of 19. From humble beginnings working for McDonald's, she worked her way to become one of the leading mindset and business strategists for female entrepreneurs in Europe today. She trains world-class women coaches and changemakers, helping them to scale their businesses to multiple six-figure incomes and beyond.

She is a professional speaker, a Neuro Linguistic Programming international trainer and a passionate believer in every woman's right to have the life and business she truly loves. Described by many of her clients as a deeply knowledgeable and inspirational trainer and coach, Lenka spurs women to action by helping them to adopt new strategies, mindsets and communication techniques, which produce extraordinary results.

As a a committed family woman and mother of three active boys, Lenka relishes the challenges her varied working life offers her.

You can contact Lenka and access her Extraordinary Growth Academy and her online resources via the following platforms:

website: LenkaLutonska.com
Email: love@lenkalutonska.com
Extraordinary Growth Academy: lenkalutonska.com/ega/
Resources: EnergeticSelling.com and
energeticselling.com/resources
including:
- *Energetic Selling Mastery Affirmations audio;*
- *Activation Meditation;*
and much more.

CONTENTS

xiv

Contents

INTRODUCTION

BUSINESS STRATEGY MEETS ENERGY

TIMES HAVE CHANGED. We women no longer want to settle for less than we truly deserve, to elbow our way through the next career goal, only to lose ourselves and sometimes our health in favour of professional success. We don't want to choose between having a thriving family life and flourishing career; or between personal and financial fulfilment; or between having a sense of purpose and a sense of accomplishment. Of course, we know we need to work to enjoy success on our terms. And so, we do. We leave the security of a job, leap into the unknown and start our own business. We roll our sleeves up and learn everything there is to learn about making it a huge success. We have spent countless hours implementing what we have learned; sometimes with success, other times wondering, 'Why can't I make this work?'

Yes, living a dream and running our own business is the most exhilarating journey any woman can take, but it can also present the very same problems we wanted to leave behind. Having to work endless hours to stand out in a crowded marketplace, sacrificing time with those people we love in favour of building a successful business, only to be underpaid at the end of the working day. The doubts creep in: 'Do I have what it takes?' or 'Can I really achieve my dream of running a hugely successful business that feeds my soul and bank account in an equal measure?' This can happen only when we rely on an action-based approach to business. We often hear the advice: 'Apply this formula and this will be your result. Take step one, two and three, and you will get this specific outcome.'

Everyone who has been in business for more than two minutes knows this is not how it works. If it did, everyone would be successful at whatever business venture they decide to pursue. There is only one element that can guarantee business success; the person driving the business. It is only when you unshackle yourself from the limits of your mind that your business can experience what you want; extraordinary growth. Your business can never outgrow your mind. I have learned this critical point the hard way. After six years of building my first coaching business, I entered an unhealthy business partnership and I managed to bring my business to the ground in a space of a few months. From what felt like one day to another, I found myself with no paying clients, no prospects, no social media presence, no website and no customer database. 'I did it once before, so I will do it again!', I told myself; and I got back to work. Building my business from the ground up for the second time proved to be a hundred times more challenging than the first time. It didn't seem to matter how much professional and business experience I had, or how hard I worked. No matter how much selling or marketing I did, clients never poured in; they barely trickled. And I *almost* accepted the never-ending struggle to stay afloat as being my new normal.

There was, however, one major difference between starting and growing my business for the first and second time: I was no longer a naïve, twenty-something immigrant worker who had nothing to lose, so why the hell not aim big? I was no longer a woman who blindly sold her house, car, and all her other possessions to fund the new business start up, thinking, 'There is no other choice than to make this work.'

I could no longer rely on youthful naiveté, blissful ignorance and taking risks larger than life. I had small kids, responsibilities and bills to pay. I knew—now—that we can be badly hurt when we take risks, so instead of naivety, I had to use courage; something I was badly lacking at the time. Instead, I overcompensated with action. Of course, it didn't really work, but at least nobody could say I didn't try. Then, one day, something crazy happened. I was sunbathing in the garden and as at many other times, I was deeply lost in a thought. 'What does it actually take for me to succeed?' I simply could not let go of the dream of running a successful business that would fulfil me in every way. A thought occurred to me: 'Well, what would you do if you didn't give a damn about what people think of you? What would you do if you were not afraid of anything?'

I started to contemplate these questions and—in what felt like the next millisecond—I received all of my answers. I knew instantly that the first thing I had to do was to stop hiding behind the mask of being a 'professional business woman' and integrate spirituality into my work with women in business. In the same millisecond I knew the exact branding message I needed to put out there; the name and structure of the next programme I wanted to offer; the pricing for my services... everything. As a result of this awakening moment and the actions I took afterwards, I sold out my first high-end group programme within two weeks! This inspired me to ask myself, 'What the hell? How come it was so easy, when I have been struggling for all those years before?'

The experience taught me that there is a deeper, wiser part of ourselves who knows not only where we want to go, but also every step of a perfect way to get there. I learned to listen to my inner voice more keenly and follow its advice in every sphere of my business to the best of my abilities, from selling, to marketing, to money management and hiring. Has it been a smooth ride ever since? Hell no. Sometimes, it was messy in the middle; but I certainly set myself, and my business on a path of rapid growth. In the space of two years I built a clientele from more than thirty countries around the globe; built a community of incredible women in business committed to make an extraordinary impact in the world; and created a sense of freedom I had longed for, for so long.

Following my intuition didn't only encourage me to make many uncomfortable decisions that went against the common marketing and selling advice; it also led me to pay more attention to energetic or, if you like, the spiritual nature of our businesses. And that is how the set of Energetic Selling and Marketing Principles and the basis for this book were born.

I have had the privilege of working with hundreds of women and helping them integrate these principles into their businesses. The results have often been nothing short of miraculous. Women increasing their fees five times and selling with greater ease than ever before; women booking themselves solid with ideal high-end clients, turning their annual income figures into their monthly income; and doubling, tripling or quadrupling their sales revenues within several months. And many times, the extraordinary change and growth has extended well beyond peoples' businesses when they start integrating Energetic Selling and Marketing Principles into their lives. My clients regularly report these results: letting go of unhealthy addictions; getting pregnant after years of trying; attracting dream relationships; and overall, living with a greater sense of happiness.

Today, I am bringing you these Energetic Selling and Marketing Principles wrapped up in this book, my dear reader. It is my desire for you to benefit and grow exactly like many women before you. These principles are certainly not a magic pill or quick fix. A strong commitment is required to fully integrate these principles into your business and life. However, I wholeheartedly believe that they have the potential to make marketing and selling your joy, and grow your business beyond your wildest expectations. This book— if you allow it—will also help you to connect with your true, limitless nature. When you do that, my darling, there will be absolutely nothing that you won't be able to create.

How To Use This Book

In Part One, Upgrade the Structure of Your Reality, I introduce you to the idea of personal energy, and you will start to appreciate how your energy affects every aspect of your business and your business results. I invite you to open your mind and I outline several universal principles that will help you to function and run your business from your higher levels of consciousness because this is where the avalanche of your ideal clients, large amounts of money and all you want live.

In Part Two, Master Energetic Selling And Marketing, I focus on increasing the return of investment of your marketing and selling activities dramatically through integrating the Energetic Selling and Marketing Principles.

5

In Part Three, Leap Into Extraordinary Growth, I guide you to re-assess how you apply your energy on the topic of money—an essential part of growth—and understand technical and energetic mechanics of creating quantum leaps in your business.

Each chapter starts with one of my business quotes to inspire your journey, and concludes with a challenge to help you implement the key learning. That is where the real power lies—in implementing and integrating the material you are about to read. I have also created a list of resources to help you integrate these teachings into your business with greater ease. Please visit energeticselling.com/resources to get your hands on them.

Lastly, for you to create greater growth in your business than ever before, you will need to—literally, not metaphorically—get out of your mind. I expect that the principles outlined in this book will stretch your logical mind and I encourage you to be particularly aware of this as you read because you may say yourself, 'This is too simple for it to work' or 'I already know this.' Please pay extra attention to passages that make you think like this; these are the gems, the treasures for you. Yes, I encourage you to open your mind wide and try these ideas, regardless of how unfamiliar they may be from what you consider normal. You and your business will reap the benefits.

> *There is no such a thing as truth. The only*
> *thing that is actually there is your 'logically'*
> *ascertained premise, which you call truth.*
> *UG Krishnamurti*

I cannot agree more. Our subjective truths influence the way we operate in every sphere of our lives. They determine our results and the same goes for our businesses. If your business is not exactly the way you want it to be, it is a worthwhile effort to re-examine your accepted premises and adopt new ones. This book will give you plenty of opportunities to do exactly that.

Open your mind, my darling, and dive in. It is time for your extraordinary growth!

With all my love,

Lenka

PART ONE

UPGRADE THE STRUCTURE OF YOUR REALITY

1
YOUR ENERGY

THE MOST POWERFUL CURRENCY ON THE PLANET

'Your business is a reflection of your energy.'

A FEW YEARS AGO a woman approached me following a talk I had given and said, 'I'd love to talk to you about possible coaching'. A few days later, we talked on the telephone to explore working together. As I listened, it was immediately obvious that I was the right person to help her. Clearly, she needed mindset coaching and this is my area of expertise. However, she shared with me her financial troubles during this call; and as I listened to her, thoughts were rushing through my head: 'Oh dear. She will certainly not be able to afford my coaching!' Before she asked me about fees, I had discounted them by 50% in my head. After all, I thought, I needed a new client, and even if she were to pay me half of my normal coaching fees, that was better than nothing. To my surprise, she wasn't excited about my generous and affordable coaching offer. 'I'll think about it,' were her exact words. Several days later, she emailed to say she had decided not to go ahead at this time. Ouch!

11

About a year later, she approached me again. This time, I proposed a coaching package at eight times the fee I had quoted previously. She pulled out her credit card and paid in full, and we entered a thriving coaching relationship. This is a real example of two sales conversations, one year apart, with very different outcomes! Exactly the same client; exactly the same needs; exactly the same coaching offer; except priced very differently. What had changed? What made the difference? I had changed and, more precisely, my energy had changed. When she had approached me the first time, I was in a place of scarcity. I was trying to rebuild my once-successful business.

At that time, as far as I was concerned, any client was a blessing. I started each sales conversation hoping that I would get it right this time. When I spoke to the same woman a year later, I was no longer functioning like that. I no longer held sales conversations with clients hoping and praying that it would work out this time. I no longer tried to prove to my potential clients that I would be the best coach they could hire. Hoping, praying, proving … you would think you can keep these things secret. After all, we think these things in our heads, and no one can hear those thoughts, right? Well, not so fast. Any form of insecurity affects your personal energy field; and your potential client will pick up on this energy, whether they are consciously aware of it or not.

Conversely, a rock-solid confidence—in your work, your fees and the potential of your clients—is infectious. It is attractive, and it sells. Your prospective clients don't trust your words; they trust your energy. You can tell them what they need to hear with your words, but you tell them everything with your energy. It is this—the energy underlying everything you do or say in your business—that makes the biggest difference to your bottom line. It is your personal energy that is the key to growing your business exponentially.

What is your personal energy?

Your personal energy is a field surrounding your body, while at the same time containing your body. It is often called your aura or energy body. It is an invisible shield of yours that introduces you before you speak. It is what quietly communicates with your potential clients on your behalf and gives them the feeling: 'I have to work with this person, no matter what!'—or it makes them hesitate. It is what gives people the first, gut impression of you, when you walk into the room. It is what you project into the web of energy that connects you with everything and everyone in this vast universe—either attracting your dream clients to you in droves, or repelling them. Your personal energy communicates with the hearts and minds of your clients. It also communicates with the divine mind. It is through this spectrum that you create your reality as you know it.

The five key elements influencing your energy

1. Thoughts: including your words, which are the amplified energy of your thoughts, and your beliefs: the thoughts which you assume to be truth.

2. Emotions: the way you feel from moment to moment, but also your stored, unresolved emotions. Emotions that were not resolved and released are stored in your energy body.

3. Values: what is important to you, ordered in priority; and how you distinguish between right and wrong, every day.

4. Awareness: what you are aware of right now; your focus and your viewpoint.

5. Actions: what you do, and what you don't do, because inaction is also a form of action.

These five elements interact with one with another, influencing each another, forever tweaking and changing your energetic field. For example, you might be focused on growing your business and looking for answers to the question, 'How can I book more high-end clients?' You come across an Instagram course, the creator of which grew her business from zero to millions in revenue, fast. 'Aaah, that is my answer!' you tell yourself. You dive into the course and find strategies you had not been familiar with before. Your belief system shifts in that moment from; 'I don't know how to do this', to 'I can totally do this! I have found my missing link!'

You apply all the learning the course suggests; except that, without you realising, what you offer is too generic, and doesn't speak to the specific needs of your clients.

No matter how much you spread the message about your work via Instagram, no matter how much time you spend building your network, your new Instagram followers are not buying your service. You start doubting yourself: 'Maybe I am not as good as other people offering similar services.' And you bring this energy—whether you like it or not—into your marketing and sales process. After a few weeks of applying this new Instagram strategy, you give up: 'This doesn't work for me. I can't make it work.' Actually, all you needed to do was to tweak the offering instead! Many women go through this cycle, many times: constantly changing what they think of their ability to sell based on the external information. Trying out new strategies, not succeeding, then developing more unhelpful beliefs that further hinder their efforts. This is what happens when we practise an action-based approach to business and let our energy—our beliefs, thoughts, awareness and actions—be unconsciously influenced as a result.

The answer to sustainable business growth is to turn this sequence on its head. It is about becoming fully conscious of what energy you apply to your business. Tweak it where you need to, so you become a complete match to your business intentions and take action from that place. It is time to stop asking ourselves; 'What do I need to do to grow my business?' and instead, ask; 'What do I need to change about myself to grow my business?' We can apply our energy on any subject you can think of: children; fashion; parenting; health and fitness; romantic relationships—you name it. Naturally, we are applying our energy differently to different subjects.

Apply your energy in these five key areas

> *'Everything that happens in your business:*
> *the number of clients;*
> *the quality of your sales conversations;*
> *the sales revenues you are used to;*
> *and the rate of your business growth;*
> *is a direct reflection of applying your energy in*
> *these five key areas.'*

1. You and the structure of your reality: what you believe, and what you know about yourself as the creator of your reality. How you feel about your ability to succeed and create anything you want. How you value yourself and whether you operate from the place of personal power, or the lack of it.

15

2. Your clients and other people: what you project onto your potential and existing clients. Are they people who respect you and love to invest in you? Or do they pay you by pressing the like button on your social media posts and praising you to heaven which, by this point annoys the hell out of you? You see, people do not behave independently of ourselves. They respond to our beliefs about them, and our actions based on those beliefs. Furthermore, it is also important how we apply our energy in relationships beyond our potential and existing clients—family members, romantic relationships, our colleagues, employees, suppliers and so on—because what we project onto them is often reflected back on us through our clients. For example, if somebody allows themselves be treated with disrespect by their children or spouse, no wonder they keep attracting clients who treat them with disrespect. Our business is a mirror to how we live our lives. It is a mirror of who we are.

3. Sales: what you believe and know about selling; how you rank selling in order of importance; how you think about it and go about it.

4. Marketing: what you believe about your ability to spread your message far and wide into the world, drawing your potential clients to you. How you feel about marketing, how you position it in your hierarchy of values and as such, how much and how well you market your business.

5. Money: how you relate to money and how much money you allow or don't allow to enter your experience, through your thoughts, beliefs, emotions, values and actions. Making more money is not about doing more. It is about allowing more.

Extraordinary growth happens when you align your energy in these five areas with that which you choose to accomplish: your business and life goals. This is when you become limitless, and this is exactly what you are going to do by reading and applying the principles in this book. You will discover how to apply your personal energy and tweak it, bit by bit, so you can become a complete match to your greatest desires in your business and life.

A great example was provided by a client called Linda Skougaard who changed her personal energy and increased her monthly sales by 500%. She had been a woman's spiritual coach and teacher for more than fifteen years. She loved her work, her clients and their transformations. All the time she was making tremendous differences to other people's lives, but she was struggling with valuing her work properly. While her coaching practice was highly successful, her business never gained financial momentum and never reached the level of impact she desired.

One day, she came across my website and downloaded every free resource she found there. She also joined my Extraordinary Growth Academy and immersed herself in applying energetic selling principles in her business. For the first time, she got rid of all her prejudices about selling. She successfully changed her energy around selling and started to really enjoy it. She embraced receiving a lot of money for her best work and started to approach her business from the place of 'I am at one with my clients. My clients are in me.' Importantly, she allowed her intuition to guide her actions. As a result, in the first two weeks of her new sales approach, she made 500% more income than she had in any other month prior to that. This experience marked the beginning of Linda's extraordinary growth journey, and opened the doors to continued growth and expansion for her coaching business ever since.

Four levels of consciousness; four ways to grow your business

A long time ago a very smart dude called Albert Einstein proclaimed, 'No problem can be solved from the same level of consciousness that created it.' This statement seems logical. For example, if you have been plateauing in your business for some time, for sure you have got to change the way you think in order to create the change and growth you want. But contemplation of this statement also brings up more questions, such as; 'What is consciousness, and how the heck do I bring it to the next level?'

However, our scientific and spiritual communities are not in agreement as to what consciousness is. Mainstream scientists consider consciousness as a biological functioning of the brain, while spiritualists view consciousness as the very essence of life, or the 'one mind' from which everything is created. While it may take many more millennia for science and spirituality to fully agree on the role of consciousness, one thing is for sure: it is simply our awareness, via which we filter—and therefore create—our subjective experience.

Peter Sage, author of *The Inside Track*, developed the model called Four Levels of Consciousness. I share this model with you below, because it not only creates a bridge between our scientific and spiritual view of consciousness, it also allows us to see it in a way that gives us practical benefits. Most importantly, you will become aware of how you perceive—and therefore create—the growth of your business and your reality as a whole. This will give you the freedom to shift it immediately.

1. To Me Consciousness

This is a victim mode. If we are honest with ourselves, each and every one of us have spent time in To Me Consciousness, and we can easily fall back into it when things don't go as we wish them to. It is all too easy to blame something or someone else for the lack of our results. Here are several examples of what we might say to ourselves when we fall into this level of consciousness:

- 'I would grow my business, if it wasn't for the fact that my family needs me more right now.'
- 'My sales flopped because people aren't buying around Christmas time.'
- 'I would invest in my growth, but first I need to wait for a few more sales.'
- 'I cannot be as successful and fulfilled as I want to be because I was born in the wrong country...to the wrong parents...at the wrong time...
- 'You don't understand!'

When we are in To Me Consciousness, we let life happen to us and react to its happenings. We let our circumstances dictate what we can and cannot do. We feel limited. We feel things are out of our control and when we don't succeed, To Me Consciousness offers us a quick explanation; it must be the fault of something or someone outside of ourselves. Simples! However, I know you are most likely well and truly past living your life through the eyes of a victim and yet, if we are completely honest with ourselves, from time to time even the best of us occasionally fall back into To Me Consciousness. Typically, when things don't go the way we want them to go; or when we feel stuck.

I recall a conversation with one of my friends when I—for the twentieth time—complained about how unlucky I was to lose my first business to a con man: 'If it hadn't happen to me, I could do x, y, z right now, but I can't do it! If it wasn't for

19

him, I would not struggle financially like I do now, but what can I do? I can't undo it! It is so hard to handle!' She listened patiently then told me what she thought.

'Lenka, listen to yourself. Poor me. Poor me. Poor me. Aren't you tired of the story yet? I don't know about you, but I am. After all, it is you who allowed this to happen to you.' Ouch. Snapping back from victim mentality into the driver's seat of our business and our lives can be a highly uncomfortable experience. It requires us to let go of any blame and adopt 100% responsibility for everything. Often, this is a hard pill to swallow. But this is also a moment when we take back tremendous power because we all have inside of us the ability to change any situation for the better. This is the moment when we make extraordinary growth possible. This is the moment when we move to the second level of consciousness and become infinitely more powerful.

2. By Me Consciousness

This is a state of consciousness where we take absolute control for our results and become a make-it-happen person. We no longer wait, hope, pray and blame. We make shizzle happen. This is what the entire personal development field is based on. 'Set challenging goals! Cultivate your determination! Never give up! You can do it!' This is also the level of consciousness where the vast majority of high achievers in business reside. Think about it—achiever equals By Me Consciousness.

There is no doubt that those people who are willing to roll up their sleeves and adopt By Me Consciousness are rewarded for it. It is infinitely more powerful to take responsibility for our results than to wait for luck, better circumstances, or someone to help us along the way. But operating through this level of awareness has also got its price. It can be exhausting. We know that all the responsibility lies on our shoulders. There is no knight in shining armour out there who can save us. We have got to prove we can do this. We have got to develop immaculate work ethics and let our determination take us through the often many obstacles to our greatest success.

'If I work hard enough, if I work long enough, I will succeed at what I want', we say to ourselves, elbowing our way through to the next career and business goal. However, many women refuse this paradigm after a while. They are tired of the transactional approach to business, the sweat and blood they need to lose to be able to get to the pinnacle of their careers. They set out on their own, starting their own ventures which not only promise great financial returns, but also will allow them to run a business their way... only to find themselves in a new environment with the same, old problems: tough competition; long hours; overcoming constant challenges; and always feeling the need to prove themselves. When we run our business via By Me Consciousness, these problems never seem to go away. However, there is another level of consciousness; and it is the one that not only helps us to stay on top of our game, but also allows us to do it with much greater ease.

3. Through Me Consciousness

This is the state known as *flow*, a term coined and researched by the American-Hungarian psychologist Mihaly Csikszentmihalyi. We enter Through Me Consciousness when we are in complete harmony with what we are aiming for. Positive things simply happen. People show up in the right place and at the right time. They call us before we pick up the telephone to call them. They open doors before we put our hand on the handle. Everything seems to be effortless, fast and easy.

Of course, each and every one of us has found ourselves, at some point, in the state of flow, and we love it when it happens. Flow makes our work life a lot easier and more enjoyable. But imagine, for a moment: what would it be like if this was your default way of filtering your reality? What if being in flow was your norm? You wouldn't only get what you aim for with much greater ease; you would flow with the river of life, which will take you to the most magical places. Of course, there would be some twists and turns along the way, but the destination would be guaranteed.

Adopting Through Me Consciousness can be a way of activating your highest potential, creating extraordinary growth, and thriving in every sphere of your life. The only problem is that most of us end up in Through Me Consciousness accidentally; we don't know how to make it our norm. So we end up back in By Me Consciousness, pushing our way forward until the next lucky break. The truth is, it is possible to consciously evoke flow in our personal and professional lives. However, the way to do that seems counter-intuitive to our logical brains. We have to give up the need for control and replace it with trust. We have to embrace uncertainty a little more. If that alarms your logical mind, be assured that by the time you have read this book, you will find playing with the field of uncertainty exhilarating. I'll see to that.

4. As Me Consciousness

Guess what: there is yet another level of consciousness, which is even more—infinitely more—powerful than the Through Me Consciousness way of living and running your business.

The As Me Consciousness is when you lean into this level of perceiving your reality and you no longer make things happen. You no longer co-create with the universe, because you know with every fibre of your being that you are the universe. You let go of the illusion of separateness and belief that you are separate from anything or anyone else. This is the state of oneness with all there is. You know that every person, thing and experience in your rich universe is a mirror image of you. It is what you are choosing. You started it all, you created it all and you are the one who is experiencing it through the infinite creations of yours, loving every minute of it. And you know that if you don't love an experience, you can choose something different. Exactly as easily as that! You will understand that you never received anything. You only gave it to yourself, and you can give yourself whatever you wish, at any time you wish. For many people, reading this may sound like an ultimate blasphemy: 'How dare I think I can be that powerful?'

The idea of accepting your infinitely powerful nature can be unfathomable or scary at first. And yet, what you find out is that the more you lean into this way of being, the more loving you become to everything and everyone in your life, and the more love you will receive in return. When you speak to your potential clients, your colleagues, friends, people you love, or to a stranger on the street, you don't speak to someone who is separate from you. You are experiencing yourself as them. You know that what you give other people, you give to yourself and what you give to yourself,you will give to other people. You know that when you help other people you help yourself and when you help yourself you help other people. You can bask in the beauty and perfection of your creation.

Adopting As Me Consciousness is incredibly good for your business. You discover that you no longer need to react to everyday circumstances, and you can decide what those circumstances are. You can practically throw away all the marketing and sales averages, because you find you can create any result in your business you like, at your will.

A great example, was Maya Novak who by leaning into Through Me Consciousness created 75% of her usual annual income in one month. She had fractured her ankle while rock climbing, and had to put up with no weight bearing for three months, and using crutches for six months. Doctors informed Maya that she would be limping for the rest of her life, and told her to get ready to live her life with arthritis: very common with that type of injury.

But Maya had a different idea. Through powerful mindset work Maya not only fully healed her ankle, she went on to run a long distance triathlon, only two years after her injury. This experience led her to start her own coaching business, helping her clients to heal their injuries, often with miraculous results. She wasn't afraid to put hours into building her business, and it worked. But it left Maya exhausted. Two years into her business, she signed up for my Extraordinary Growth Academy saying to me, 'It's my time to make a much bigger impact in the world!' She told herself that she would give it all of her focus for six months, and only then would she measure how effective the Energetic Selling teachings were.

Within the first month, she completely changed the way she approached her work. She reduced her working hours by 50%, which was extremely uncomfortable for her to start with. Instead, she dedicated more time to her own interests, her own self-awareness and understanding, and the application of a more energetic approach to business. What Maya said happened next was miraculous.

'Visits to my website doubled from one day to the next. At first, I thought it was a glitch, but it remained that way. I also created my best month ever in business. But the next month was even better, a lot better. In short, in one month –three weeks to be exact, as I also took holidays that month—I realised that I created 75% of my previous annual income. The best part was that it happened with complete ease! As I discovered, by adopting a higher level of consciousness and an energetic approach to growing my business, it is much easier to make a lot of money by doing less. Everything simply flows.'

It is my intention, expectation and knowing that as you read through the pages of this book and choose an energetic approach to your business, you will be more and more able to access the same higher levels of your consciousness and remain there for longer periods of time. This will save you months, even years of By Me Consciousness action, when it comes to achieving your most ambitious business goals. You will live by knowing that your energy is the most powerful currency on the planet and you will be able to change it instantly and with it, what is happening in your business and life. Perhaps even more importantly, you will step into a higher version of yourself in the process. You will become who you need to be, to be able to create miracles in your business and life and that is priceless.

EXTRAORDINARY GROWTH CHALLENGE:
THE I AM WALK

THIS PRACTICAL EXERCISE may feel strange at first, but it is a fantastic way to start practicing As Me Consciousness. Take a short walk around your neighbourhood. Notice your surroundings and with everything you see, tell yourself; 'I am that. I am.' Feel into the knowing that the life and energy that flows through you, also flows through that tree in the distance; the rock you step on; the stranger you meet; the bird singing; the air you breathe; the sun you soak up; and even the pile of rubbish you may walk past. Feel into the knowing that all of this is a product of your consciousness. It is your projection, your creation and you are not only creating it; you also are it. If you are up for it, extend this exercise to your home and office. When you talk to someone, acknowledge that you are talking to a reflection of yourself, to yourself. In your mind, run through the list of your suppliers, clients and your colleagues; and as you do, say to yourself; 'I am that. I am.'

Practising this will help you to start letting go of the stubborn idea of separateness. The chances are that you have been running your business under the illusion that you are separate from those people who you wish to serve; that you are separate from the money you want to enjoy; that you are separate from experiences you want to have. Tuning your awareness into the idea that 'I am one with everything I perceive' will help you to overcome this illusion. In return, it will mould your reality to exactly what you want, and attract perfect-for-you clients—and anything else you desire, for that matter—with much greater ease. Why wouldn't you allow yourself to experience what is already yours, that which is you. Right?

IN THIS CHAPTER YOU HAVE DISCOVERED

- What is your personal energy.
- How your personal energy influences the results you achieve in your business.
- The importance of tweaking the way you apply your energy before you tweak your business strategy.

- The four levels of consciousness and how to move from the lower levels to a higher level and as a result grow your business with much greater ease.

Before you move onto the next chapter, ask yourself the following questions and if you wish, journal about them. Reflecting on these questions will help you integrate what you discovered in this chapter and start the process of extraordinary growth.

1. 'Out of the four levels of consciousness—To Me, By Me, Through Me, As Me—which is my default way of perceiving and creating my reality? Do I wish to change this? Why?'
2. 'Which of these five areas—me and the structure of my reality; other people; marketing; sales; and money— will require me to change how I apply my energy in these areas, in order to see the growth in my business I require?' Take into account your current business results and patterns when answering this question.
3. 'How would I like to see my business reflecting my energy in these five areas?' What is your ideal when it comes to how your potential and existing clients respond to you, your marketing, selling and your money? How about your relationship with yourself, and your beliefs about creating the reality you desire?

In the next chapter, you will be introduced to the aspect of your personality that will turn these ideals into your experience. We will move you from feeling limited to being limitless. Let's do this!

2
YOUR HIGHER MIND

THE MOST QUALIFIED SALES COACH AND GROWTH STRATEGIST

'Your higher mind contains a blueprint of your full business potential, and it is constantly revealing the fastest path for its fulfilment to you, through the images, impulses and feelings of desire you receive.'

'REMEMBER, YOU ARE WRITING for the top 1% of business people in the world.' Those were the words of the editor-in-chief of *The Billionaire Chronicle,* a quarterly printed publication distributed to various royal offices and many of the wealthiest people in the world, after approving my idea for a feature.

'No bloody pressure!' I thought to myself. I reserved a generous amount of time—most of my working day—to write and submit the article on time. My deadline was in three days from that email exchange. However, after four hours of working on this specific article, I hadn't written a quarter of what I wanted to say. I was having a real dilemma, with doubts circling around my busy mind: 'They may not relate to this.' 'This might sound too woo-woo for these readers.' 'This is too basic!' These were the unhelpful thoughts taking me away from the keyboard and off to make another round of coffee. It was seriously hard work.

The next day, I facilitated an Implementation Session for my VIP Mastermind clients. It was 90 minutes of focused work, where my clients complete an exercise which moves them forward in their business in leaps and bounds. I thought to myself, 'I had better not be a hypocrite and spill my beans.' I told my clients that their coach was going to move her butt too. I was going to finish the article in the next 90 minutes. I sat down at my computer and before I typed the first letter, I told myself, 'Screw this. I am giving myself permission to write this article in my voice and give them my truth. If the editor of The Billionaire Chronicle likes it, fantastic; if not, I am not meant to be writing for them.' Ninety minutes later, the article was finished and submitted. I nervously awaited the feedback from the editor: 'I love your article, thank you!' Boom! I was so happy! This story is totally relevant to you; my little writing shenanigan is a perfect metaphor for how we operate in our businesses. Let me explain.

Physical mind versus higher mind

At any given moment, we have two different parts of ourselves interacting with each other: two different states of being, and two different aspects of our mind.

The first is our conditioned mind, which is our ego-self; the local, programmed and physical mind. It has many names and I often lovingly call it our lazy mind. This is the part of ourselves where everything is familiar to us. All the books are on the right shelves. Everything is predictable. The name of the game for this part of ourselves is order. It is the thoughts we are used to thinking, the words we are used to using and the actions we are used to taking. It is everything, which has brought us to where we are now.

It is also the part of our mind that gives us the illusion of separateness; the left hemisphere of our brain sees to that. It is the most important function of your ego-self. This illusion of separateness, however, can be both a gift and a curse. Gift, because that is the only way we can experience this beauty called life. Curse, because that is the only reason we often feel limited; without or with few answers; empty; stuck; and scared. Our physical mind loves linear thinking and following a step-by-step plan for achieving your next financial goal. By Me Consciousness is where this part of our mind likes to be. It simply loves familiarity and logic. Above all, your ego-self wants to keep you safe. It doesn't want you to be hurt, disappointed, judged or criticized. It whispers to you: 'If I do this, how will it come across to other people? What are the dangers of doing this or saying that, in this way?'

It is lovingly looking after you. The only thing is, your ego has no understanding of what exists beyond it; it has only theories. And it sees threat in everything, and treats you like an overly protective mother: 'You should not do this or that, my darling. You are okay as you are. Stay here.' This aspect of your being loves the feeling of accomplishment, but if it needs to choose between growth and avoiding perceived danger, it always chooses the latter. If this aspect of your mind is not attended to and negotiated with, it will keep you and your business smaller than you can be.

The second aspect of ourselves is our higher mind, our higher-self, our potential. It is that part of you which is forever nagging and whispering to you; 'This is who you are meant to be. This is who you can become. This is what you can have.' This is the field of creation out of which all the ideas are born. Your higher mind represents chaos and the unknown. But it doesn't perceive itself in that way. For unlike your physical mind, you higher mind is not limited by any programming such as unhelpful beliefs; and it also has a concept of 'all there is'.

Through your energetic body, your higher mind is intimately connected to the web of energy that bathes the entire universe. It sees the whole picture, and has access to solutions your lower mind simply doesn't have. What your ego sees as uncertainty, your higher mind sees as the field of infinite possibilities. This part of you holds the fuller version of you and it constantly reveals itself to you through the images, impulses and, most importantly, desires you receive. Your higher mind will say, 'Come this way, it is going to be worth it.' Your physical mind will argue, 'Don't go there. It is too risky. It is unpredictable.'

For example, your higher mind will nag, 'You can have the success in business you want, health, that amazing relationship, and time for yourself.' Your ego-self will reply, 'Success comes with sacrifices. Don't aim for too much, otherwise you will be disappointed.' Your higher mind will remind you, 'Be you and give yourself to the world. You are the most important asset of your business.' Your ego-self will doubt it, 'I am not good enough for that.' Remember, the extraordinary growth you desire requires you to commit to the guidance of your higher creative mind, more often than the guidance of your physical conditioned mind.

Moving from being limited to being limitless

Now you have brought into your awareness the main functions of your lower and higher mind, the 'how' of creating quantum leaps in your business becomes obvious. The fastest path to your extraordinary growth is to think and act more as your higher-self and less as your ego-self. It is about moving beyond the fears, doubts, and uncertainties we experience as a result of associating ourselves with our ego-self; and instead, leaning into a way of being that is in alignment with our highest potential…when anything becomes possible. Simpler said than done, I know!

The good news is that extraordinary growth of your business doesn't require you to altogether let go of ego and everything that is associated with it. No, a level of predictability is healthy, as long as it is not what we are seeking predominantly. It's exactly the same as an Olympic athlete pushing the boundaries of what is possible for them physically: we too can explore and lean into what is possible for us. And this, my darling, starts with awareness. You want to become conscious of internal dialogues between your ego-self and your higher-self, rather than react to these dialogues on autopilot, like the vast majority of people do. You want to become aware of who the heck is talking right now, and who it is more worthwhile to listen to.

Higher-self thoughts versus lower-self thoughts

If you are actively working on growing your business—rather than staying put in your comfort zone—there is no doubt you will experience these internal dialogues between your higher and lower-self very often. Perhaps multiple times a day. For starters, this dialogue takes place every time you have an opportunity to grow. Let's say, for the purpose of an example, you have received an inspired idea to launch a brand new service or product for your existing audience. You are giddy with excitement, which is, by the way, always a good indication that this idea was offered to you by your higher-self. You are imagining how this product or service will benefit your clients; how much fun it will be to bring this to completion; how it will benefit you personally. Then you start considering the details. You start looking into what should be the exact features of this service. You instinctively know, but you say to yourself, 'Let me have a look at what other people do...to make sure I am right.'

You browse the Internet, and find that five other people are offering similar services and they are more popular with bigger audiences and they have already priced their service cheaper than what you intended. 'Okay,' you say to yourself. 'I need to price this more cheaply than my competition.' You adapt your pricing accordingly and you discover you need to sell three times more to make this as profitable as you wanted. 'Hmmm, but I am not sure if I have enough people on my mailing list to sell this to so many people and if I charge what I originally thought I would, who would buy it anyway? Let me sleep on it.' In the morning, you think; 'What was I thinking? This was a stupid idea!' And there you go, asking yourself 'How can I grow my business faster?' with yet another unimplemented inspired idea. This is not necessarily because you got a wrong idea to start with, it is because you engaged your ego in the process too much, without questioning it.

Does this sound familiar? Have you experienced something like this? Of course you have. I am sure you can relate to little or big fights between your ego-self and higher-self, as this scenario demonstrates. Your higher-self is always propelling you forward. It is always giving you guidance as to what is the next step to take to grow, only for your ego-self to argue with it and reason with you because it wants to keep you safe. Here is the thing: these fights are good, healthy and essential for your extraordinary growth, provided you let your higher mind win more often than not. The trouble is, most entrepreneurs do not distinguish between the talk of their ego and of their higher-self. Instead, they assume they are confused.

Let's make this very clear. Yes, both your ego-self and higher-self communicate to you through your thoughts. These thoughts may even sound like you. They may feel like you. We follow our thoughts unconsciously, taking everything as a fact. And yet, this is the biggest lie. Thoughts, whether coming from your ego or your higher-self, are not true in their nature. All thoughts—ideas, concerns, risks and considerations—are simply energy. I will say it again. Your thoughts are *not* true. Your thoughts are not you. Every thought you ever thought of, every thought you will ever think of, already exists as a cluster of energy. You do not create your thoughts. You attract them. As such, you can decide which thought you associate yourself with— take it as your personal truth—or reject it. Of course, we want to accept those thoughts that are communicated from your higher mind, rather than your lower mind. But how do you recognise which one is which?

Well, a great start is to ask yourself, 'Who is talking right now, my ego or my higher-self?' The best indication, however, is the way they feel. In other words, the feelings behind those thoughts show you the way. Every time. You see, higher-self thoughts feel expansive; exciting; sometimes exhilarating because they are in perfect alignment with who you really are. Ego-self thoughts feel restrictive. They will give you a physical signal in your body—a negative emotion— most often the feeling of fear.

Please remember this. When you feel any form of negative emotion, especially fear, it is a physical signal that you are associating yourself with the ego-based way of thinking. In that moment, you are accepting something that is not in alignment with who you really are. This is the only reason why these thoughts do not feel good because you are buying into lies!! When this happens, instead of taking it as a warning when your ego-self shouts, 'Danger, danger, danger!' accept it as an extremely good sign. This negative feeling is an invitation to shift your awareness from your lower self to your higher-self. It is your invitation to stop buying into lies and explore your truth, to explore how your higher-self sees and act accordingly.

'Are you telling me to stop running away from fear and go towards it instead?' Pretty much, yes. You see the function of the fear has never been to protect you. The fight and flight instinct does that for you. Fear—or any other negative emotion, for that matter—is an indication that right now, you are letting your ego-self be functional. You can feel fear only when you are accepting ego-thoughts as your truth. Once you shift your awareness to your higher-self, once you start thinking as your higher mind is thinking, fear will quickly turn into excitement. And once you follow your higher mind's guidance, in spite of the fact that your ego-self is scared—it always will be—more often than not, you will grow; and your business will grow with it, faster than you thought possible. We could argue that it is the fear—or arguments of your ego-self—that are showing you the greatest opportunities for growth. Never disregard them simply because they make you scared. Explore them, thoroughly. It is freaking worth it.

A perfect example is the case of Lovelda Vincenzi, who stepped into the unknown and turned her life around completely, positioning herself as a leading expert in her business niche. She started by stepping into the New Year with the thought, 'The only thing that I will do this year, apart from my corporate job, is MC-ing.' This is something she had a huge passion for. 'If I can make £10K from this side-gig this year, I will be happy. It would be a great start', she shared with me during our first sales conversation.

But it turned out that, deeper down, Lovelda wanted much more than that. Given the opportunity, she would love to resign from her corporate job and focus not only on MC-ing, but also on helping other women get on big stages. She shared her frustration with me: 'When I MC events, I introduce male professional speakers 90% of the time, as if women don't have a voice, which is of course, not true at all!' And it was immediately obvious that Lovelda could achieve this, and much more.

But, first things first; she needed to learn to by-pass her logical, lower mind: that clever mind of hers which was responsible for many of her corporate achievements so far. She signed up for my VIP Mastermind Course with the intention of doing everything in her power to release into the world the beast of a woman entrepreneur she knew was dwelling within her. 'I had to learn to listen to the other part of me, my higher-self and become more aware of the fights between my higher and lower mind', she told me later. Within six months, she achieved many things her logical mind was fighting against, but her intuition encouraged her to do.

She opened a Facebook Group for speakers, in spite of 'never liking Facebook groups and certainly never having a desire to run one' only to find that it effortlessly attracted ideal clients her way. She put together and sold out female speaker conferences, in spite of the fact that she 'didn't want to organise events—it is a hard business model'; and the conferences were not only huge successes, but introduced Lovelda to many influential people. She followed her intuition, and pitched during the first female conference, in spite of the fact that her ego was telling her, 'You don't have enough authority to offer your services; only speakers on the stage can do that.' As a result, her first high-end Mastermind Course, through which she helps speakers to find and get booked and paid speaking events, was a sellout.

This is the feedback she gave me: 'In six, short months, I completely turned my life around, in ways I never imagined was possible. I resigned from my corporate job, because my new business afforded me the opportunity to do so. I got on international stages, introducing some of the biggest names in industry, and I created new courses that now help many speakers around the world. But launching my first VIP Mastermind Course was my proudest moment so far, because it happened as a series of events that would never have happened if I had followed only my logic. It goes to show how powerful it is to follow your inner guidance, step into the unknown, and sometimes say 'Yes' to things before you get too scared or rational.'

The language of your higher-self

> *'Think for yourself.*
> *Trust your intuition.*
> *Another's mind isn't walking your journey.'*
> Warren Buffet

In case you need a reminder, Warren Buffet is a man who increased the value of his company, Berkshire Hathaway by an astonishing 751,000% in 50 years. And it turns out that Warren Buffet is not the only business mogul who relies on the power of intuition to create extraordinary growth in business. A study of 13,000 business executives by Harvard researcher Jagdish Parikh showed that they credited their intuition for a staggering 80% of their business success. And there is no wonder why; intuition is how your higher mind communicates with you at all times.

As we already established, your higher mind has access to a far wider web of information than your lower mind does. It communicates knowledge to you via intuitive guidance. Your intuition can truly be the greatest sales coach and business mentor you can ever hire, given you know how to work with it. Personally, I dedicate time and effort to not only learning about intuition, but most importantly—strengthening it—learning to trust its guidance. I am not shy to admit this has been the most important business tool, which has grown my impact and my business.

There are five things you need to take into account when you want to power up your intuitive intelligence:

1. The more you listen, the more guidance you receive

We are all receiving divine guidance. There is no question about it. But some people can 'hear it' more easily than other people. The good news is that we can all work on opening up this communication channel and making that inner voice louder, so to speak. How? By simply listening. For example, including listening time—even as brief as three minutes—in my daily morning routine has worked wonders on how easily I can receive guidance. Simply ask yourself, 'What is my part in this?' As in, achieving your goals with ease; or overcoming a specific business challenge; and then, listen. Note down all the ideas that come into your mind, no matter how crazy they sound, no matter if you think you are making it up. Take each piece of information as it is given to you. Sometimes you will receive lots of ideas, other times you will get nothing. It doesn't matter. Simply listen. The more you do this, the clearer and more frequent the voice of your inner genius becomes.

2. The intuitive ideas you receive are always a perfect match to your energy

Yes, we can receive inspiration both from lower vibrational states—such as anger, fear, and so on, and from higher vibrational states such as excitement, belief and love. If you feel stuck, needy or desperate and you are looking for guidance from that place, you might receive inspired answers. But guess what? Applying that guidance will give you more of the feeling of being stuck, needy or desperate! Attend to your vibration before seeking answers from your higher-self. If you want to receive clarity on solving a particular problem, focus on the feeling of having answers, or a feeling you experienced when you were crystal clear the other day, rather than focusing on 'I am confused and have no idea what to do, help me out here.' If you want to receive intuitive ideas to create extraordinary growth in your business, visualise what that extraordinary growth looks like for a few minutes, and notice how you feel as if you already achieved it. From this emotional place, you will be able to receive divine guidance more easily, and the ideas will be a perfect match to creating the extraordinary growth you desire.

3. Intuition is a whole-brain function

Your intuition is filtered through your physical mind. Let me describe how incredibly intelligent and complex this process is. Have you ever walked into a strange environment and immediately got a gut feeling about it? In the millisecond you entered this new environment, your higher mind integrated all the following aspects of the situation.

39

a) The input from all-that-is: the infinite web of possibilities, which your lower mind has no access to.

b) The input from your five physical senses: what you see, hear, touch, smell and taste.

c) Programming of your lower mind: your entire life experience, knowledge and beliefs.

This is why learning about your craft and especially practicing your craft is incredibly useful when it comes to being able to receive intuitive guidance that will lead to your greatest growth. This is also why it is so important to work on yourself; your personal energy. Because, let's say, if the programming of your lower mind is, 'No matter what I do, it will never work', your higher mind can scream and shout at you all it likes, but you won't be able to hear it.

4. Relaxed state enhances your intuitive hearing

Thomas Edison, one of the most celebrated inventors of all times, had a famous napping habit. Several times a day, he rested sitting upright in his office chair while holding steel balls in his hands, with metal saucers directly underneath them. He contemplated solving a particular problem, and his body relaxed to the point that he involuntarily dropped the balls. The sound of the balls hitting the metal saucer immediately woke him up. He then promptly noted down the ideas he received during this half-awake state. You see, as you relax and your brainwaves enter Alpha and Theta states, you calm your ego-self; you get out of your mind, so to speak.

This is the best state of consciousness to communicate with your higher-self and receive the guidance you seek because it is when you are closest to it. You don't need to develop a complex napping routine like Thomas Edison did, but it is worthwhile to allow yourself to get out of your mind often and listen for intuitive guidance in that state. For many people, a brief visualization or meditation will do the trick. For others, it will be dancing, or walking in nature. Whatever relaxes your mind, use it as a doorway to the infinite wisdom possessed by your higher-self.

5. Intuitive ideas often don't make sense at first

Your higher mind is the highest form of intelligence and it holds energetic data ripe with potential to transform your world and fulfil your highest potential. It knows far more than your logical mind knows. As a result, it is only natural that your intuitive guidance will often sound illogical. When intuition hits, refrain from judging the idea solely based on how much sense it makes; instead, evaluate it by how it feels. If the idea feels expansive and exciting, you can be assured that it is your higher mind talking and it is surely a worthwhile exercise to explore your idea further. Be careful though. While it is okay to evaluate your intuitive ideas using common sense, you don't want to invite your ego-self to the party: 'How will I come across?' for example, 'Will I be rejected?' or 'Will I fail?' These are considerations your ego-self might offer you while you examine your inspired idea.

Get to know your threshold between following your inspired ideas and being foolish. Then, stretch that threshold. For example, in the last three years of running my online business, I have done many seemingly foolish things. But I did these things and I continue to do so, even if the ideas I receive often don't make full sense to my logical mind. Even if I am seriously scared at times, I keep choosing 'foolish' any time my intuition tells me to do so. At one point, I closed my three offline entrepreneurial networking groups, my only source of regular income at the time. On multiple occasions,

I launched programmes and offerings that to my logical mind were 'too cheap' or 'too expensive', or 'too out-there' and I did it to test the validity of intuitive knowing.

I can tell you that my intuition has never failed to deliver. Looking back, every applied intuitive idea—no matter how crazy—was an important step towards enjoying the business success, and everything that comes with it, which I enjoy today. So, excuse me if I say that 'this is too foolish' should not belong in the vocabulary of extraordinary entrepreneurs and change-makers and certainly not be an excuse to disregard our ideas. 'Am I foolish enough?' is a much better question to ask ourselves!

A good example here is Tatiana Fecikova, who followed her intuition and increased her personal income by ten times. She lived a typical migrant life: working in a pub, cleaning people's houses, and babysitting whenever possible. Her life was ticking along, but she dreamt of doing something more meaningful. 'On the inside, I was like a dead person,' she said to me. In spite of the fact that she didn't have any saved money, and it made zero sense logically, she signed up for my high-level Mastermind Course with a strong intention to find herself—and that she did.

Over the course of two years, Tatiana followed every hunch and bet on herself many times—scary as it was—regardless of what her friends and family kept telling her: 'Don't be crazy!'and 'You'll fall flat on your face!' She started her own business and quickly established herself as a go-to-person for high-level online entrepreneurs who wanted to implement money making systems and structures into their businesses. She increased her personal income ten times in two years, working half the hours she used to. She cleared all her debts and upgraded her lifestyle massively, allowing her to travel internationally any time she wanted: something she had always dreamt about, but didn't think it was possible.

Of course, with Tatiana's new energy and approach to life and business, there were other changes she never expected, one of which was attracting a dream partner into her life. This is what she told me: 'Following my intuition is scary as hell at times. My ego has been showing its claws at me many times over the last few years but doing what I know deep down is right for me has paid off a thousand times. I will continue to bet on myself and follow my intuition, no matter what.'

EXTRAORDINARY GROWTH CHALLENGE: LISTENING MEDITATION

THIS MEDITATION WILL HELP YOU strengthen your intuition. For best results, practise daily. This particular meditation has three segments, which are best practised in three-minute intervals. You can prolong them later, if you are called to do so.

Interval One: Releasing

Invite fears and doubts to surface.

As they come to you, become aware of each unhelpful thought pattern, such as:

- 'I don't have enough time to implement my idea.'
- 'If I go for this, I will have to sacrifice a lot.'
- 'I may fail.'

Imagine writing each fear on a piece of paper.

Acknowledge that this fear is an indication that this thought is a lie.

Acknowledge that this thought is not real, nor the only option; it is simply an energy. Say to yourself, 'I see you. I acknowledge you. I release you.'

43

See the paper with the fears written on it disappearing into the distance or being burnt on a fire, whatever suits you best.

Repeat this process—acknowledging and releasing—with each fear that surfaces.

Interval Two: Higher-Self Activation

For three minutes—or longer if you wish—visualise achievement of one of your intentions. Imagine it has already happened; you are the person who already did that, the person who already has that. You are already that person you want to be, right now. Notice as many details as you can and most importantly, notice how it feels having achieved what you desire.

Interval Three: Listening

Ask yourself, 'What is my part in this?'

What is your part in achieving this intention with ease?

Stay still and listen.

Be open to receiving intuitive guidance.

Whatever comes to you, take it as it is given.

The more often you do this process, the louder and clearer your intuition will get; and that, my darling, is priceless!

IN THIS CHAPTER YOU HAVE DISCOVERED

• The difference between your ego-self and your higher-self, and how they interact with one another and influence your every action.
• The true nature of fear, and how to use it to create quantum leaps in your business growth.
• The importance of intuition on your path to extraordinary growth, and how to strengthen it.

Ask yourself the three following questions before you start reading Chapter Three.

1. So far on my business journey, which part of my mind have I let myself be influenced more by: my conditioned mind or my higher mind?
2. What have been the consequences of this, so far?
3. What are three examples from my life when I followed my intuition and later reaped benefits?

My darling, you are getting to the place when you are ready to create extraordinary change in your business and life. We will do that in the next chapter!

3
YOUR PERSONAL CHANGE

THE FASTEST PATH OF EXTRAORDINARY GROWTH

*'You are either creating change, or postponing change.
There is no in-between.'*

MY FATHER—as many caring fathers do—designed my life for me, in detail. 'You will learn five languages. You will study banking and finance at one of the most prestigious universities in the country. You will have a decent job.'

But I had a different idea. All I wanted was to change the world, and no matter how stupid or crazy this idea was, I was going to make it happen. The year I was supposed to start university, I hopped on a bus heading to London, with £30 in my purse. We learned at school that London is a cosmopolitan city where you can make your dreams come true—music to my ears! Thankfully, a family with two small kids were awaiting me when I arrived. I became their au pair, and I learnt English in my spare time. Unfortunately my au-pair career lasted only three weeks. I was terrible at it!

I found myself walking from shop to shop on a high street in an unknown town, asking strangers, 'Do you have any jobs?' People at McDonald's must have felt sorry for me, and in spite of my broken English they gave me a job as a customer care assistant: a fancy word for a cleaner, but it was okay because I was one determined chick. It wasn't long before they had no other choice than to promote me—again and again and again. Soon enough, I became an award-winning business manager, managing hundreds of people and millions of pounds in annual turnover. I bought a house and drove a fancy car, and life was good. I studied a lot; I took counselling, hypnotherapy and integrative psychotherapy courses—you name it. I got my hands on anything I could find to learn about the human mind and find a way to be able to work with people in some way and to… yes, you guessed it… to change the world!

Coming across Neuro-Linguistic Programming gave me all the answers I needed. I sold my house and my car, left the job and departed for Sydney, Australia to get myself trained to the highest level as an accredited NLP coach and trainer.

I came back to the United Kingdom, broke as hell but full of enthusiasm about my future. I started a training and coaching business from my then boyfriend's—now my husband's—kitchen table. I gave it all I had, and it worked. Soon enough, people were attending my NLP courses from all around the world—entrepreneurs, doctors, scientists and business executives—and my private coaching practice was thriving too. I was living my dream, changing the world, one person and one group at a time. My business was thriving and growing, and I started a family with my husband.

Six years into my business, however, I made one giant mistake and entered a business partnership that went sour. As quickly as I had built my business, I lost it all in a few short months. I ended up with no client database, no website, no social media presence and no money. I still dreamt of changing the world; but clearly I had to change my world first. Going back to a job was not an option for me. Instead, I thought, 'I've done it once, I'll do it again.' So, I gave it my all, once again. I worked practically every waking hour. I was one busy woman!

But being busy and productive is one thing, and actually growing is an entirely different thing. While I got myself out of my biggest debts and could at least pay the household bills again without constant worry, I continued to wonder why the hell my coaching business was not growing in spite of me working for it like a dog. Then I got my answer in an unexpected way.

One day I met a client at a beautiful manor house for a coaching intensive. We asked a staff member to take a few pictures of the two of us together before we left. My client sent me that picture a few days later and when I looked at it, I froze. I saw a beautiful, confident woman—my client— proudly standing tall and smiling to the camera; confidence was oozing out of her. Next to her was me: a woman elegantly dressed, a woman who had spent three hours coaching that other confident woman, helping her with strategies for the next level of her business growth. Except, I was crouching, tilting my head down, with my entire physiology making myself look small. I thought, 'Wow, I look so small in this picture, so insecure!' It looked like I was the one that needed a good amount of confidence coaching! And there was my answer. I was making myself small.

This didn't reflect only in this picture, but in every area of my business. I undercharged for my services. I kept proving to myself and to other people what an amazing coach I was, but I never really owned how good I was, nor confidently pitched for my services. I wasn't willing to take any more entrepreneurial risks. After all, I had lost my entire business the last time I took risks! Except, I didn't really lose my business because I took a risk: I lost it because I didn't believe in my ability to take my business to the next level. I wasn't feeling good enough for it. Yes, I was practicing To Me Consciousness in relation to expanding my business; a way of thinking that can be truly detrimental to business growth.

I stared at that picture for a good few minutes, and knew instantly that the answer to growing my business was in my willingness to play a bigger game. To stop pussyfooting around and start walking boldly towards what I wanted. To stop playing safe because I had fallen flat on my face once; instead, to bet on myself. And that was what I did. In the following days, weeks and months, I made a series of changes that made me highly uncomfortable: from changing my pricing structure; through to changing my marketing message; to investing heavily in high-level coaching and business education. The rest, as they say, is history. Yes, the moment when I committed to my dreams more than to being safe was the moment when I activated my extraordinary growth, and the extraordinary growth of very many people, my clients, with it.

You see, the steps towards creating a business you will truly love will not be terribly complicated. In fact, even if you take the most complex tasks, such as landing a rocket on the moon, even that can be split into many simple steps. When it comes to creating extraordinary growth in an online coaching business—an industry I am very familiar with—the process is really quite simple: make sure you have a marketing message which is focused on solving your ideal client's needs; create coaching offerings based on your marketing message; put proven marketing systems into place that are aligned with you, whether it is through paid advertising, public relations, or other methods, so your ideal clients can get to know you;

49

nurture your clients with good content so they learn to trust you; and sell your services every day.

Sure, this process can be broken down into smaller segments and steps, but none of these steps is particularly difficult. What makes it difficult, however, is the chatter of our conditioned minds. What makes it difficult is practicing To Me and By Me Consciousness. Most importantly, what makes it difficult is our unwillingness to change. You see, there is no doubt about this one—the extraordinary growth you desire will require change—a lot of it—on your part. The woman who already runs the business you are dreaming about; the woman who earns loads of money by doing what she loves; the woman who is growing her impact exponentially; will be the same woman you are today; except, she will have different ways of thinking; different habits; and different internal strategies.

EXTRAORDINARY GROWTH CHALLENGE: HABITS OF THE NEXT LEVEL YOU

I ENCOURAGE YOU to stop reading right now. Grab a notebook and explore how different you would be if you already ran the next level business you dream about. Doing this will make reading the rest of this chapter much more meaningful for you. Allow yourself to go there, right now; to a time and place when extraordinary growth is your norm. Visualise yourself already there and answer these questions.

- Who really is this woman?
- What does she do from day to day?
- How does she think?
- How does she approach her marketing and selling?

- What is her relationship with money?
- How is she relating to her clients?
- How is she going about growing her impact further?

Compare the new version of this woman with the one you are being today.

- What is different?
- What do you need to change?

The chances are you may not be aware of everything you need to change and that is okay. One thing is for sure, you will realise that if you want to create extraordinary growth in your business, you need to change a few things about you. Perhaps the next level you is about trusting yourself more. Perhaps, she is more ballsy and courageous. Perhaps, she is more visible to her prospective clients. Perhaps she sells her services much more. Get the idea?

I don't know: only you know these answers about you and your business. What I do know however, is that no matter what changes you need to make, that change will be simple in its nature, but far from easy. Writing a book, for example, requires developing a daily writing habit. You need to sit down and start typing your thoughts down for an hour, or whatever writing time you decide is needed to write that book. Every day. There is nothing difficult about that! The trouble is, it is also easy not to do it. It is far easier to get distracted and do something else instead, make excuses and postpone writing that book until later. Yes, I am saying this from my experience! You see, our brains are not designed for us to change easily.

In his book *Change or Die*, Alan Deutschman describes extensive studies of patients who underwent bypass surgery, a traumatic procedure relieving chest pains temporarily, but not preventing heart attacks or premature death. When these patients were warned that they must change their lifestyle or risk death, you would think all of them would change immediately. Not so fast: only one in ten patients adjusted their lifestyle to prevent another painful surgery or premature death. Whoa! Think about this for a moment. If you were given a choice between changing your lifestyle dramatically, or dying prematurely, you have only a 1:9 chance that you would actually change. Not a very promising statistic, right? Why is that? Why is it so hard to change?

First and foremost, it takes far less mental energy to do habitual, repetitive tasks than to do something new. Most of our daily activities, including our working habits, are controlled by a part of our brain called the *basal ganglia*. Think of it as automatic brain. For example, one study[1] showed that in any given day, we think anywhere between 12,000 and 60,000 thoughts; and 95% of our thoughts are exactly the same ones we thought yesterday! Yes, the comfort zone is very sticky!

Creating a new habit—such as daily selling, book writing, live streaming, operating from the belief; 'I am good enough' and so on—pushes us out of our comfort zone by stimulating the prefrontal cortex: a section of our brain connected with reasoning and conscious decision making. The trouble is, the prefrontal cortex is also connected to the most primitive part of our brain, the *amygdala*. This part of our brain does not think rationally; it controls our fight-or-flight response, and it reacts on autopilot. When your prefrontal cortex is overwhelmed with a new task and with unfamiliarity, your *amygdala* kicks into a higher gear. It makes you feel uncomfortable. It awakens your ego, encouraging you to back off: preferably, right now.

52

---

[1] The National Science Foundation

This is why so many entrepreneurs can stay perfectly stuck at one place, not being able to smash that proverbial glass ceiling, for weeks, months, even years. They follow what is scientifically known as the natural process of change. They take a few steps forward, outside of their comfort zone with new actions and into the uncertainty zone, only to retreat back again. Then they take the same actions again at a later stage and retreat back, but not as far forward as they went the first time. So they advance, as we say, 'one step forwards, two steps back'.

We are perfectly able to pussyfoot between where we are and where we want to be forever. Until...something bad happens. You are made redundant or go bankrupt. Or simply get to the point where you feel so freaking awful about where you are, that you are not able to tolerate one more minute of it. You experience a kind of push or pull that creates a real urgency to change. That place is highly uncomfortable. But that is also a moment when we have no other choice but to change. It is a moment when the pain of going through the change is smaller in comparison to the pain of staying the same. From there, the only way is up and towards the desired, permanent change. Yes, extraordinary growth!

A brilliant example was my client Sarah Ann Negus, who left a comfortable multi-millionaire lifestyle and reinvented herself as a spiritual multi-millionaire. However, she was no stranger to going through the discomfort of change. One day she decided to resign from her perfect life, owning several seven-figure businesses with her husband, living in a gorgeous house and having a great social network. As good as this life looked from the outside, Sarah was completely empty on the inside.

One day, when the pain of living this fake life was too much to bear, she walked away with a single suitcase, her children and a dog. She didn't even have her own bank account. Now while this was certainly a gruelling process, she rebuilt her life the way she wanted. Several years down the line, not only had she manifested a new, fulfilling relationship but she found herself running a successful business as—brace yourself for this—a modern day shaman, working with entrepreneurs to activate their highest potential. The change was worth it. But Sarah wasn't quite done yet. Her business, while successful, was going through feast-and-famine periods and she had—frankly—had enough of that.

Once we started to work together, Sarah was very quickly—in fact during the first call—able to own her brilliance. Instead of proving to other people how valuable her work was, she prospected and sold with unbreakable confidence. And within the first week, she signed ten high-end clients. But that was only the beginning. She also had to learn not to work so hard, something her conditioned mind wanted her to do. You see, it had been her sheer hard work that had led her to her previous successes. These days she says, 'When you slow down, everything speeds up. I had to remind myself of this mantra that Lenka gave me many times, while I was developing the habit of working smart and in a more centred, truthful way, rather than working harder. And indeed, it worked.'

Sarah went on to build a wildly successful, ever-growing coaching business. She is now regularly invited to speak on big stages and deliver corporate workshops, and her 1-2-1 coaching is highly in demand. In addition, she started several other entrepreneurial ventures, one of which secured her spiritual multi-millionaire status. Change is not easy; but it is the exact thing that will take you to your greatest highs as an entrepreneur, creator and an influencer.

Cheating your brain and activating your extraordinary growth

Thankfully, you don't have to wait for bankruptcy, redundancy or divorce to be able to commit to change yourself in a way that extraordinary growth in your business becomes inevitable. Instead, we can cheat our brains and take these four actions that make the change process much more likely.

1. Stop settling

The impulse to settle for where we are is a powerful, invisible force holding us prisoners to our fears. We settle when we talk about being committed to growing and changing, but never putting our money where our mouth is, never really changing, but rather postponing the change. We settle when we think how much we want to improve and change things, but every day we tolerate not changing them instead. To stop settling, we must come face-to-face with the real cost of not changing. We must make it clear—not only on a cognitive level, but also on emotional level—what is the real cost of remaining where we are today. This, while an uncomfortable process for many people, creates strong urgency to change: an 'away from' effect in our neurology, so to speak. We humans are fascinating creatures. We are much more motivated to avoid pain than to gain pleasure. When it became clear to me, by looking at that photograph of my client and myself, just how much I was settling for less than who I could be, and how it was hurting me, my clients and the people I love: that was exactly what I needed to get off my high horse and start taking those uncomfortable yet meaningful steps forward. I simply stopped settling. Incidentally, this is why, whenever I am asked the question,

'How long does it really take to grow a super successful business?' my answer is always, 'As long as you tolerate not having it.'

2. Set powerful intentions

A few years ago, shortly after that infamous 'oh-shit-look-so-small' photo moment, I attended an in-person event for entrepreneurs. During that event, we were asked to share with a small group of attendees our biggest business dreams. I replied, 'I see myself running VIP events for women coaches and entrepreneurs in a luxury environment; empowering them; and helping them to change their lives. I see it. I don't know when, or how, but I know it will happen.' One of the women in my group asked, 'When would you like to make it happen?' My answer was 'Hmm, I'm not sure! It might be possible somewhere between five to ten years.'

About a year later, I found myself painting an old piece of furniture in my garden. A few weeks prior, I had given birth to my third son and for some reason, I developed a fetish for refurbishing old pieces of furniture while I was 'nesting'. Don't ask why—I have no idea! I ran out of stuff to re-paint at home, so I went and bought this old cupboard so I could paint it. There I was, listening to music, applying paint to the cupboard and enjoying myself. At that time, my business was in a much better place than a year earlier. Much better. My business was fully online; I grew a tribe of wonderful followers and paying clients; I loved everything about my business.

But that image of running luxury events for women entrepreneurs was still a 'one day' type of idea, as was the idea of running a seven-figure business that changes many lives. Suddenly, a bizarre thought occurred to me; 'What am I waiting for?' I dropped the paintbrush, ran inside our house and screamed at my husband, 'How will you feel if your wife becomes a millionaire? Are you okay with that?' Confused and with a somewhat cheeky smile on his face, he replied, 'Do whatever makes your heart full, my darling. Of course I am okay with it.' 'Good!' I said and ran into my office. I can't remember exactly what work I did that day. But what I remember was that from that day onwards, I was working on and in my business from a new level of energy; with more conviction, more self-belief, more umpf. Two months later, the cupboard was still sitting in my garden, half-painted. Instead, I had a first group programme launch, where I created £100K in contracted sales within three weeks: at the time, a huge amount of money, and a massive leap in my business.

A few months afterwards, I ran my first exclusive event at a luxury hotel for women entrepreneurs. That event was an exact replica of the picture I had carried in my mind and it all happened in eighteen months as opposed to five to ten years. But in fact it happened when I dropped that paint brush and run into my office. That was the moment when I was not only aware of what my higher-self wanted of me, but when I fully accepted it. That was the moment when I set a non-negotiable intention instead of thinking what I wanted was 'a thing of the future'. I call this 'owning your desires'. No matter what you call it, this is an important step towards making whatever change is necessary to make your extraordinary growth happen. We will go deeper into this concept in the next chapter, so that you can come to the place where you make the miracles you are looking to create in your business not only highly possible, but inevitable.

3. Repetition
Once you identify how you need to change and the cost of not changing, and own your next level potential, you will be ready to make the required changes. That bit is, in fact,

instant. The moment you make a non-negotiable decision and do something different from what you normally would in the direction of your goals, your brain will start creating new neuro pathways. Every change is instant. There is no process of change. You are either changing, or postponing change. There is nothing in between. The trouble is, your neuro pathways associated with old habits of thinking or doing, never really die. When under strain or challenge, your brain will automatically choose the strategy—or circuit, if you wish—that has been rehearsed more; the one that is harder wired, so to speak. That is why the repetition of your new chosen behaviour or way of thinking is required.

For example, if you identified that one of the changes required to experience extraordinary growth is to prospect on a daily basis, but you have been avoiding prospecting like the plaque up to now, it is not enough to change your beliefs about prospecting. It is not enough to wake up one day, prospect for three hours and celebrate. You need to do it every day, even if for only five to ten minutes, my darling, until you do it on autopilot. This is the same with any habitual way of thinking or feeling. It is not enough to decide once that you are worthy of success, even though in that moment you upgrade your consciousness and your physical brain with it. Technically, in that moment you changed, but you still want to reinforce the change.

First, you will want to integrate this new decision by exploring and running in your mind, how will this new decision affect your everyday business activities. How does the belief, 'I'm worthy of success' translate into selling, marketing, money management and so forth? You will want to explore this, and ideally run the new behaviours in your mind in detail. For example, if you identified that one of the 'I'm worthy of success' behaviours is to confidently state your fees during sales conversations—without justifying and forever talking about how your fees are worth it—you will want to have this type of new, upgraded sales conversation in your mind often. Yes, there is a tremendous power in mental rehearsal. Numerous scientific studies have found that a combination of imagined practice and actual practice result in better performance than those achieved with preparation that relies solely on actual practice. But of course, actual practice is very important too. With the example of, 'I'm worthy of success', you want to practice selling from that place repetitively, until that connection in your brain is so strong that, even in your weakest moments, you don't think yourself out of your power.

4. Get support

Daily training of your new you with repetition, however, carries new challenges. There is no doubt that it will awaken your ego, on more than one occasion; that you will be doubting yourself while reinforcing your new ways of approaching selling, marketing, money and other areas of your business. That is why having a strong support is essential. Form a relationship with a coach, plus a community who will inspire your constant growth and change and support you in making extraordinary growth happen. Just as the sun doesn't know how hot it is, or a knife doesn't know how sharp it is, we have no idea how powerful we can be, or how easily we can sabotage ourselves because we are too associated with ourselves. We are inside of ourselves. Having a coach and a community who can see you from the outside perspective, can catch you when you are falling into your 'old' self, will listen to you when you need to be heard—and will challenge you to always, always keep changing and growing—is the most beneficial business relationship you can have.

Here is the thing, my darling. While it is perfectly possible to create quantum leaps in your business fast, you want to make this growth sustainable. You don't want to have one great month or one great quarter, hoping that things will stay that way. You don't want to be a one-time wonder. You want to be a woman for whom extraordinary growth—again and again—is her second nature. And for that, you will want to have that outside perspective. Always, just like an Olympic athlete would never dream of going for the gold medal by themselves. You too deserve having a coach and support network behind you as you walk the never-ending—and extremely exciting—journey of extraordinary growth.

A perfect example was Corinne Worsley, who transitioned from burnt-out executive to booking high-end coaching clients with ease. She was a high-flying IT and finance consultant. She was able to 'tick all the boxes' before the age of 30—six-figure salary, house ownership and a beautiful car. Except that, while pushing her way through never-ending and extremely demanding working days, she developed adrenal fatigue and had a breakdown. She had known that something had to change, and needed to change immediately. She left her job and explored various other options. She wanted to help other people; have a location independent career; and she wanted to make good money.

After exploring her interests and skills, life coaching turned out to be a natural choice for Corinne. For one year, she tried building her coaching practice. She experienced success here and there, but all in all she did not create the momentum in her business that she desired, and her savings were running short. She was losing faith in her ability to build a successful coaching business. She joined the Extraordinary Growth Academy, a group coaching experience for women entrepreneurs, which in her own words, she found invaluable. 'For the first time, I committed to my dream more than to my fear. I developed courage and had enough support to do things that were highly uncomfortable for me, but essential for my business growth. I learned to prospect every single day. I delivered my first webinar, in spite of the fact that my conditioned mind was telling me, 'It is going to flop. Nobody will sign up.' I stopped doing only things that came easily to me—such as writing amazing blog posts and creating valuable videos—that had ultimately left me waiting and hoping for my next client. Instead, I became highly proactive. My ego was fighting with me every day, but I developed enough conviction to keep going.'

In the first month after joining the Extraordinary Growth Academy, she booked four high-end clients, which not only made a huge difference to her bottom line, but gave her even more conviction that she indeed could build a wildly successful business. 'None of these new clients had any objections about my high-end fees. My new clients all wanted to pay in full. This showed me what a difference a non-negotiable decision, commitment to change and strong support network can make.'

IN THIS CHAPTER YOU HAVE DISCOVERED

- Why and what is necessary for you to change to create the extraordinary growth in your business that you desire.
- The natural process of change.
- How to cheat your brain and make your change and growth inevitable.

Before we move onto the next chapter, journal your answers to the following questions. They will help you to integrate the first step in activating your full business potential. You will face the real impact of staying where you are right now and the cost of remaining the same.

1. Where am I settling for less than I really desire?
2. What do I need to change about myself to grow my business the way I desire?
3. What is the impact of not bringing about this change? What will it cost me—during a five year period—to settle for remaining the same: emotionally; mentally; spiritually; physically; and financially?
4. What am I changing right now?

Take focused time to answer these questions, deeply. Do not rush this exercise. While you may find answering these questions uncomfortable, the benefits of being honest with ourselves is tremendous. It will get you off your butt, and that is always a good thing when it comes to creating quantum leaps in business. Most importantly, it will help you commit more to your growth than to your fears; and that is when you open the doors to miracles!

4
YOUR AWARENESS

THE ONE THING THAT CHANGES EVERYTHING

*'What you experience at any given moment is just a tiny
fraction of what is possible for you.'*

'IF YOUR MIND can conceive it and believe it, then you can achieve it.' You have probably heard this quote on a million-and-one occasions, in a million-and-one versions; full credit to Napoleon Hill for this thought. Having interviewed and studied 500 millionaires and many of the biggest business minds of his time, he knew what he was talking about. Typically, we don't have a problem with conceiving ideas or business goals; that is the easy bit. Our higher-self is one stubborn lady and she continually knocks on our mind, showing us who we could be. It is easy with those goals within the boundaries of our comfort zone. Or, perhaps, just outside of it.

The trouble is that these kinds of goals have hardly anything to do with extraordinary growth. The name of the game is to believe you can do things that are far beyond your normal and believe it so strongly that no internal self-talk and no unfavourable circumstance or failure you might meet can

63

change your mind. In fact, you don't want to simply believe you can do it. You want to know it.

You never affirm to yourself, do you, that: 'I believe I can walk from my living room to my kitchen!'—a hundred times a day while looking into your eyes in the mirror and pumping your chest? You don't need to do that, because you simply know you can do it. Knowing is the next level of belief. It is a state of being that will help you achieve your business intentions and the extraordinary growth you desire, faster than you thought was possible. Knowing can turn even what was once impossible into your here-and-now reality.

I am sure you have experienced the power of such belief before. For me, the first time was when I decided I was going to become an American Board of NLP accredited trainer with a 100% certification score. ABNLP is the largest and oldest certification body for NLP in the world, and I knew that if I wanted to use NLP professionally, I needed to study with them. But I was told that it could not be done: 'Nobody from the United Kingdom has ever achieved a score of 100%. It is a very demanding certification.'

But I had a different idea. I sat down and wrote an intention for myself, creating an image in my mind of achieving my goal, winking at my NLP teacher, the person who told me it couldn't be done and saying, 'I told you!' I decided this image was to become my reality, and I got to work; I studied with great concentration and focus. I also needed to become very good at presenting, and I needed the money to afford the course and for the reality of studying in Sydney, Australia. I was enjoying a decent salary at the time, but I did not have any savings and my goal required a substantial financial investment! 'Never mind,' I thought to myself, 'I will work it out.'

I bought a flight to Sydney on my credit card, and set out to attract funding for my studies. Deep down I knew that getting certified would be the beginning of my journey as an entrepreneur; the beginning of my new life. I put together a business plan and visited half a dozen banks with a request for a business loan. Unfortunately, none of the bank managers shared my big vision. No was the answer, every time. Lastly—and this would surely be a detail, I thought—I needed to sort out a visa. In practice this was not at all straightforward. My passport was apparently not valid for long enough to grant me entry to Australia. It was not such good news one month before the flight to Sydney; and the money for the training still wasn't there.

The fact that I had resigned a month earlier and had hence lost my income didn't help either. I remember thinking, 'I am fooling myself,' because it seemed nothing was working in my favour. But I continued to study. I went to my home country and got myself a new passport and I tried to persuade my friend, with whom I owned a house at the time, to re-mortgage it and let me sell my half to her. After a week of talking, crying and begging, she agreed. I sold half of my house to make it happen, and the money from the bank, as well as my new shiny visa, arrived only a few days before the flight. Wow!

Incredibly, once I graduated, I experienced in reality the image I had been holding in my mind for months, with every detail: the way they announced my name when I indeed achieved the 100% certification score; the feeling of immense pride and excitement flowing through my body; and winking at my trainer, uttering, 'I told you it was possible!' Incredible things can happen when you make up your mind; when you set powerful intentions; when you own what you desire. I am sure you have experienced this in the past, perhaps on multiple occasions. Now, my darling, it is time to apply this to your business. It is time to go beyond believing. It is time to know with every fibre of your being that no matter how crazy or impossible your new intentions might be, you can own them fully and actively work on making it your reality. How do you do that? How do you develop such strong beliefs about something that is as far out of your normal as it can get? There is only one answer to that: by appreciating how powerful you are.

'Our deepest fear is not that we are inadequate.
Our deepest fear is that we are powerful
beyond measure.'
Marianne Willamson

What follows are the principles that govern our universe and the process of creating our subjective reality. I personally revisit these principles often, especially when my conditioned mind questions, 'Can I really do this?' You will find that when you open your mind to make these principles your personal truth and act as if they are your truth, you will become far more confident in your ability to create miracles in your business and life; and very efficient in manifesting what you desire. It is possible that these concepts may be far away from what you know to be true, and that they challenge your belief system, as I mentioned in the introduction. Despite this, I now invite you to go down a rabbit hole with me, my darling, and let's stretch your model of the world, so that you can accept exactly how powerful you really are.

Everything is energy

That chair you are sitting on; the clothes you are wearing; the amazing book you are reading right now; that wonderful body of yours: these appear to be physical but they are not. 99.99999%[2] of whatever you are looking at is an empty space, and if you took all that empty space out of our human bodies, all 7.5 billion of us, you could fit what remains—pure matter—into a single sugar cube. That is right: you can fit the entire human race into a sugar cube!

But how do we appear physical? Well, our bodies have this incredibly intelligent mechanism through which they can decode vibration. What we 'see' is not all there is, but is decoded information in the form of light; and we are blind to everything else that exists. There are many other known forms of energy that exist, here and now, that are just as real—such as X-rays, gamma rays or FM rays—but we are not able to see them. In fact, we are able to see only 4% of the known energy forms, and these represent only about 0.05% of all the energy forms in the universe. If you do the maths, you will need to acknowledge that our body is designed to show us only a very limited version of reality; and even what we do experience via our senses is, in the words of Albert Einstein, 'merely an illusion, albeit a very persistent one.'

Moreover, there is no difference between what we call matter and energy. Matter is energy vibrating at a frequency that can be decoded by our physical senses.

Think about this: everything is simply energy vibrating at different frequencies.

'There is no empty space, but rather intelligent energy responding to your thoughts and feelings.'

What we call emptiness—the stuff between visible parts of the universe—is not emptiness at all. According to quantum mechanics, it instead contains fleeting

[2] Joe Dispenza, Breaking the Habit of Being Yourself

electromagnetic waves and particles that pop in and out of existence. Our universe is bathed in a field of intelligent energy, and this fills all emptiness. It also bathes not-emptiness; and in that from, it behaves or vibrates differently. We have this intelligent field that penetrates through everything and everyone you can think of. Additional scientific discoveries[3] show that this field responds to us—rearranges itself—in the presence of our feelings and beliefs.

You are connected to everything and everyone else

Each of us is like a wave in the sea of energy that is this vast universe. The wave in the ocean may seem separate to the eye and you would not be able to tell where one wave ends and where the other one starts. The wave is the ocean and the ocean is the wave: as it is with you—you are seemingly separate from everything and everyone else—yet you are the same stuff that bathes the furthermost corners of the universe and penetrates through all the people, rocks, animals and plants. That stuff is one super-intelligent, all-powerful mind. Exactly as each wave creates ripples in the ocean, you too create ripples in the universe with your intentions, reorganising an entire pattern.

One of many wonderful examples of this principle is the power of group meditation. In 1993, researchers led by John Hagelin, a renowned quantum physicist, successfully conducted a carefully controlled scientific experiment[4] in Washington DC, studying the effect of a large group of meditators on social trends. The idea was to show how easy it is to reduce crime and social stress by using group meditation to intervene from the field of consciousness. The researchers predicted that the crime rate would reduce by

[3] Greg Braden – Spontaneous Healing of Belief, 2008 (Hay House)
[4] Effects of Group Practice of the Transcendental Meditation Programme on Preventing Violent Crime in Washington, D.C. July 1993, D.C.Institute of Science, Technology and Public Policy Technical Report 94:1, 1994. Social Indicators Research (vol 47 issue 2, 1999)

20% in the city during this experiment. They were met with ridicule from the local police officers. In fact, the police chief went on record to say that the only thing that would reduce crime to such an extent in Washington DC during the summer months would be twenty inches of snow. The researchers went to work.

Between 800 and 4000 trained meditators participated in a group meditation during this period, and the results were quite astonishing. During these eight weeks, the crime rate fell by as much as 23%. The statistical probability that this result could reflect chance variation in crime levels was less than 2 in a billion. In other words, it was confirmed beyond any doubt that group meditation had a tremendous impact on the behaviour of specific people living in the city. Since then more than 40 other similar scientific studies have taken place and confirmed the accuracy of this finding, and the power of group meditation.

So next time you think your thoughts don't affect anyone else, think again. You will find this principle useful when asking yourself the question, 'Where can I find perfect-for-me clients?'

Time does not exist

The only place where time matters is in the human mind. If you ask your dog, 'What time is it?' It would look at you in a funny way and answer, 'It is now, silly!' We humans have a different idea though. We agreed that we will think in minutes that are 60 seconds long and months that are anywhere from 28 days to 31 days long, and years that are as long as it takes for our earth to orbit around the sun. We are also the only beings that can project ourselves into the future.

However, what if time doesn't exist at all? Think about this for a moment. Why do you think time exists? For most the answer and justification is because things are changing. Everything is constantly changing; our bodies, nature, the weather etc. But is this change caused by time? Or is the change happening regardless, and we just use time to measure it? If you think about it for long enough you will probably come to the conclusion that the latter is a more reasonable explanation.

Our bodies, for example, don't get old, but rather become more used. You can have a 1965 car that is looking and functioning like a brand new car because the owner hardly ever drove it and looked after it very well. Or it can be a dysfunctional wreck because it was used on a daily basis. Unlike cars, we cannot choose not to use our bodies, so they gradually deteriorate. But it is not because of time. With time we only measure how our bodies are changing. But if there is no time, what is there? There is only one infinite moment of now, where everything that ever happened, could happen, or might happen, is existing all at once. Everything you might consider in your past—the one you experienced, or the one you did not—also all your possible futures: these are all an infinite number of configurations of the universe existing in one infinite moment of now. Only one of these configurations is active at any one time—your here and now experience—but all of these configurations exist. They exist as potentiality or as something that vibrates at various vibrational frequencies, which your senses are not decoding right now.

Think about this a little more. Your next level business potential—the extraordinary growth you desire to create—is not 'time' away from you. It is not 'space' away from you. It is already here and now; it is in you. The only reason you are not experiencing it yet is that you are not decoding that particular frequency. In other words, you are not accepting that particular configuration of the universe as your reality. 'Tell me how do I do that!!', I hear you shouting. Let's go a little further down that rabbit hole together now, and have a look at how we create our here-and-now experience.

How we create our subjective reality

Your consciousness, or awareness, behaves similarly to electrons orbiting around a nucleus, the basis of all existence. It switches between a localised and de-localised state. You could say that your awareness goes in and out of existence. It is like a light switch going on and off very very quickly. Each time it switches on—many times per nanosecond—it makes active one particular configuration of the universe. The next configuration you experience might be very similar but never the same. This happens so fast that we have a perception of continuity—time. And yet one configuration of the universe is completely independent from another. By the time you drink a cup of water, you may switch between trillions and trillions of these configurations: various different realities.

Think of it like a movie. It is made of a huge amount of pictures projected onto the screen. The pictures are changing so fast it seems like it is a continuation of the same thing. But it is not. You can cut the movie into separate pictures and take one to France and the other one to Sweden and these pictures can exist independently one from another. And yet, when projected one after another, in a certain sequence, voila, you have a movie. Going with this metaphor, each picture is a particular configuration of the universe. It is a picture that is infinitely more rich and complex than a single slide of a movie to the point that you cannot imagine it with your physical mind. But stay with me and let's explore this metaphor further.

Right now you are in the middle of one movie. You are projecting the slides of this movie onto the screen and your body is translating it in to your here and now experience. There are different movies available though, an infinite amount of movies. Movies are made of infinite pictures or infinite configurations of the universe, infinite realities. When you contemplate this for a few minutes, and dare to accept this as your personal truth, you will not escape the conclusion that what you experience in any given moment is only a tiny fraction of what is possible for you.

Now, if you desire to create extraordinary growth in your business, this is a different type of movie. That movie—your preferred reality—will look different. So if you want to have that movie projected on the screen of your life, you better get clear on what you want it to look like. Let your imagination run wild. Create it and see it in your mind exactly as you want it to be and decide that this is the only version of reality you are accepting as your truth. Make that powerful intention, right now.

Now that movie will have a different vibrational frequency. In other words, it will feel different. Simply ask yourself, 'How would I feel if I already had what I wanted?' Whatever comes up—ease, fulfilment, expansion, fun, or something else—this will be a good indication of the vibrations you want to practice to become a perfect match to that version of reality. You want to choose that particular emotion now. For example, if the underlying feeling of the reality you want to create is freedom, then choose freedom now. You can do it in two ways.

Firstly, notice instances in your everyday working and personal life when you are free: for example, you have freedom to choose what to eat. You have freedom whether to walk, drive to work, or take a bus. Look for the instances that you normally overlook. If you acknowledge them, they will give you the same feeling you will have if you already had that next level of the business you desire.

Secondly, choose activities and experiences that embody that feeling. For example, if running gives you a feeling of freedom, do it more often. If employing an additional team member in your business would give you more freedom, do it now. While these actions can take you out of your comfort zone, you are choosing energy that is the basis of the reality you wish to experience. And the universe cannot do anything else but reflect it back on to you. It will have to give you more freedom, in terms of money and clients, and much more— you name it!

Emotion is energy in motion, and the more you choose the emotion that represents the achievement of your juicy business goal, the faster it will become your here-and-now reality. What you choose chooses you. But it is up to you to choose it first.

Awareness changes everything

If you wish to watch a new movie, you have to watch that movie, right? It would be a little silly to watch a drama and complain throughout the whole movie that you would have preferred to watch a comedy. Yet that is what we often do in life. We dictate what is happening next, which slide we project next, by what we observe and by what we are aware of. And that observation, my gorgeous, makes all the difference. In the quantum physics world, this phenomenon is called the *Observer Effect*, which states that 'simply observing a situation or phenomenon necessarily changes that phenomenon'. On a subatomic level, for example, we know that mere observation of electrons influences how that electron behaves. It can act both as a wave and as a particle. If not observed, it will act as a wave. But if there is a measuring device, for the purposes of tracking the journey of these electrons, something strange happens; electrons collapse from wave function into particles. If you are not familiar with the now famous Double Slit Experiment, which beautifully explains this Observer Effect phenomenon, I encourage you to look it up and absorb it. The universe responds to you in exactly the same way. Depending on what you observe, you will be decoding your vibration of reality, which is a natural continuation of that movie you are watching right now.

When you want to shift your reality, you have to shift your awareness. You have to watch a different movie, regardless of what your current reality looks like. Stop taking cues from your current circumstances as to how to feel and what to expect next. Instead, make up your mind about what you want to experience and imprint it in your mind and heart. Live in that reality to as much extent as possible. The next time you go for a walk, don't go as the woman you are today. Go as the next-level you. The you who already created that extraordinary growth in her business; the you who has it all. The next time you communicate with your audience, don't do it as the woman you are today. Do it as the woman you want to be tomorrow.

Overwhelm your current experience with your preference. See what you want to see. Hear what you want to hear and, most importantly, feel what you want to feel. Your current reality is extremely malleable. It is simply a result of what you observed and therefore thought and felt yesterday. Today, observe differently. Think differently. Feel differently. I appreciate that this can be tricky at first, because of course there is a time delay between the stages: setting a powerful intention; making up your mind; observing your new reality; and having that chosen reality actually show up in your experience in its fullness. At times, it may feel like watching a movie that normally makes you cry, and instead of crying, laughing as if you are watching a comedy.

What is happening around you and what you choose to see may not match, at first. But they will. They must, because the moment you set the intention and the moment you decide to see only that and nothing else, the universe will go into overdrive to deliver this to you. In the very moment of making a powerful intention, you start downloading the vibratory pattern of that particular configuration of the universe.

This conscious observation is one way you can focus your mind and cut years off the timeline between where you are today and where you want to be in your business. It will collapse your timeline, so to speak, and allow you to enjoy what you desire much faster. Am I encouraging you to be delusional? Pretty much. Take your awareness to what you want to experience until the line between what is 'real' and what is 'fantasy' starts to become thinner. For example, I used this way of focusing myself when I was in between my two businesses. I was broke, but wanting to launch my second coaching business. At one point, I developed a new and rather strange morning routine when I was walking my two young boys to school every day, which took six minutes each way. After I had dropped them at school one day, I decided not to walk home as the same woman. No, I walked home as the woman who owned a quarter of a million pound business. I said this phrase quietly in my mind, 'I am an owner of a quarter of a million pound business.'

In reality this was as far from what I considered possible at that time as it could be because I was totally broke. Nonetheless I focused on my new business intention and I noticed how it felt. I asked myself, 'If this was really true right now, if I was really an owner of a quarter of a million pound business, what would be different?' As I was thinking about it, I realised that not so much would be different on the outside. I would be wearing similar clothes and I would be walking with my kids to school, but I would carry myself differently. I would certainly feel different; and that was how I was walking home from school, carrying myself and feeling like a quarter of a million pound business owner.

I cannot tell you exactly how long it took me to build a quarter of a million pound business since my New Me Walks. Looking back, it happened very fast. But this exercise took off many months, if not years, of continual struggle, and it helped me to build and continued to grow, the business I so deeply love, much faster. And it could not have been otherwise; because for six minutes a day I chose to be a perfect match to the reality I wished to experience. I was feeling rich and powerful inside, in spite of the fact that my coaching diary was crying for more clients and my bank account was crying for more money. For six minutes a day I was overwhelming my current experience with my chosen preference. I simply ignored everything else. I became that woman. Although it was only six minutes a day, this profoundly affected the way I was feeling, thinking and acting for the rest of that day. I was more focused, I had better ideas, and I became more productive.

And so it will be with you, my darling. Once you decide to embody the woman you will become when you run that next level business, the universe must take notice. That is the definition of watching a different movie. When you watch a different movie and make yourself a vibrational match to your chosen, new reality, things will be happening so fast for you that you will be pinching yourself. Hooray!

Your next level business already exists

In a way, you are never creating anything. You are merely letting what you desire to emerge from the non-physical wave function to the physical. That preferred reality of yours—although you are not seeing it here and now—already exists, exactly as everything else that you can think of already exists. The only question is: will you choose to experience it? If the answer is yes, start observing it today. Embody that energy, overwhelm your current experience with your chosen reality. Watch that movie. Even if it is only for a few minutes in your day, it will cut many working hours from your working week, because the entire universe, with all of its angels and fairies, will be assisting you and your business will so love it.

EXTRAORDINARY GROWTH CHALLENGE:
NEW ME WALK

THIS EXERCISE WILL HELP YOU practice your focus and direct it into your conscious observation. Go for a walk as a woman who has already achieved your most ambitious business goals. From the moment you leave your home until you return, embody the woman you would be if you had it all. Walk as that woman. Think as that woman. Feel as that woman. You might want to repeat a phrase, or a series of phrases, that you wish to call into your reality, such as these examples.

- 'I am running a multiple, seven-figure business that changes many peoples' lives.'
- 'I am a bestselling author of my first book.'

Never treat these phrases as mere affirmations, though. Take them as they are: as true, right here, right now. Don't project yourself into the future: rather, bring into today what you want to experience in the future. Be that woman when you take that walk. Enforce your preference on your current reality and as you do that, open yourself to receive new ideas and opportunities, listen to your intuitive guidance. For the best results, do this daily!

IN THIS CHAPTER YOU HAVE DISCOVERED

- The extraordinary growth you desire is not time or space away from you. It is in you.
- You don't create your reality. You create conditions for your preferred reality to emerge from the non-physical to the physical.
- Time becomes malleable when you understand it is a mere illusion, a mind filter that allows you to have human experiences.
- Belief is good. Knowing—in other words embodying—this chapter's principles is a lot more powerful than belief. It is a state of mind that creates miracles.

Before we move to the next part of this book, *Master Energetic Selling and Marketing*, journal your answers to the following questions.

1. What is the underlying energy of my business? Hustle? Flow? Something else? Define it.
2. What is the underlying energy of your next level business? Freedom? Ease? Define it.
3. Based on the answer to question number two, think about various ways how you can notice that energy—emotion—in your everyday life, and how you can choose it more often.

Okay my darling. You are ready to own your next level potential. In this very moment, things are already shifting for you. In the following chapter, we are going to make sure that you can attract perfect-for-you clients with ease.

PART TWO

MASTER ENERGETIC
SELLING & MARKETING

5
ENERGETIC MARKETING

*'Your perfect-for-you clients are not separate from you.
You are connected to them right now, more intimately
than your logical mind can comprehend.'*

I DON'T NORMALLY parade my children in front of my clients, but there was an exception. My husband had to travel for his dear grandma's funeral, leaving me with my three boys in daily childcare and an active business to run for a week. My little one, at the time a two-year-old, had zero interest in childcare and decided to be stuck on my lap for an entire week. He missed his Dad, bless him!

Perhaps because of added pressure, I went through a few days of 'energetic shit storm'. For seemingly no reason, I was questioning every area of my self-worth as a woman, entrepreneur and mother. I didn't give up on my audience and business altogether, though. I did a couple of live streams and wrote one newsletter, pouring my heart out, writing about challenges I was currently going through, how I was dealing with them and how we all can use our challenges to propel us forwards. That single email inspired three women so much they reached out to me to talk about my 1-2-1 coaching. I talked to two of those women while my little one had a nap. With the third sales conversation, I wasn't so lucky; I did it while my little one was sitting on my knee.

In the middle of that storm, I created more than £50K worth of business and some new gorgeous paying clients, all in one day. Two of those clients had known me for less than seven days and they had only recently 'accidentally' discovered me. I felt like a superwoman that day and I was questioning, 'What the hell? £50K days as a coach are not supposed to happen this way?'

But you see that is according to the old marketing books. They tell you that you need to have a million-and-one elaborate marketing funnels; spend ten hours a day on social media; and convince anything that breathes to buy from you. With the energetic approach to marketing and selling, you can throw these books away. It is not uncommon in my experience that a single inspired action—such as that one piece of writing for my audience—can bring amazing results. That is because true connection—what you are aiming to create through your marketing efforts—transcends time and space. It transcends the boundaries we create in our minds: 'I only have this many people on my mailing list. I only have this many people following me' and so on. It transcends all of that. That is what Energetic Marketing is about. In this chapter, I will answer one of the most persuasive questions on every entrepreneur's mind: 'Where can I find my dream clients?', and explain how to attract them with ease.

Where can I find my high-end clients?

I cannot tell you how many times I have been asked this question. It is a valid one; yet, when you think about it, the very question comes from an erroneous assumption that we and our clients are separate. The question is based in By Me Consciousness. Sure, it is worthwhile to study where your ideal clients hang out. Consider where they gather online, offline, what they listen to and read, and where they go and find help to solve their burning problem. Show up for them in those places. But beyond basic research and common sense, it is also worthwhile to stop telling ourselves how disconnected we are from those people we want to serve:

'I feel like I am in a pond, and my high-end clients are in the ocean. I don't know how to get there.' These are the words of one of my gorgeous clients.

We create these metaphors in our minds, and they keep us away from tapping into the limitless nature of our connection. It used to be, in the old days, that you were connected to every person on planet Earth through up to six other people; it used to be called 'six degrees of separation'. This is no longer valid. Facebook connected us so well that you are only 3.5 introductions away from any other person on the planet. Think about this for a moment—you are connected to any other person in the world through a maximum of 3.5 people. Yes, you already are connected to perfect-for-you clients.

But energetic connections go deeper than that. In Chapter Four, we talked about the energetic field that penetrates everything and anything in the entire universe. You are bathed in the same intelligent energy field as your clients are; that is what connects you at all times. Therefore, your thoughts and marketing actions have the ability to reach your client's minds and hearts across the globe, as long as you are opened to that idea. Think about this: a simple Facebook post, as long as it is set on 'public', can reach pretty much anyone. Of course, you could argue that you would need a hell of a lot of luck to reach the right people, but that would mean underestimating the power of your intention, and your As Me Consciousness.

I cannot emphasise enough the importance of taking a common-sense action, such as showing up to your ideal clients where they naturally gather. Generally, whenever I hear the question, 'Where can I find my high-end clients?' My answer always is: 'They are everywhere. Where are you?' Think about these powerful questions.

- Are you showing up for your clients? Or are you hiding, because you are not sure what to say or what other people will think of you?
- Are you being of a massive value to your clients? Or are you struggling for ideas of how to let your genius shine?
- Are you giving your clients an opportunity to get to know you? Or are you hiding your one-in-the-whole-world personality behind the words and marketing tactics that 'should work'?
- Are you communicating the same brand message every time you show up? Or is your message vague and ever-so-changing?
- Are you making offers? Or are you trying to be fully booked without selling?'

The truth is that those clients you desire to serve are not some-place; they are intimately connected to you. They are a reflection of your consciousness. They *are* in you. They are you. Once you can accept this as your absolute truth, your internal guidance will open its floodgates with new ideas for your marketing. Your marketing efforts will not only bring better returns on investment for you. Oftentimes, you will be amazed how easily you can attract those perfect-for-you high-end clients. You will have a feeling that it is happening for you, rather than having to work your butt off 24/7 to spread the word about your work.

For example, Heidi Plumberg—an Extraordinary Growth Academy participant—excitedly shared with the other people in the group: 'Yesterday I noticed one woman on social media sharing her problem. I felt inspired to offer her advice, so I did so in the comment section of her post. The next thing I knew, there were hundreds and hundreds of people requesting to join my group overnight!' Many of these people who accidentally saw Heidi's comment, and accidentally liked it so much that they checked this coach out, joined her group and actually became her paying clients. Later on, Heidi became recognised as the founder of one of the fastest growing companies in her country, Estonia. She didn't do this via action alone; in her own words, 'That would be impossible'. She did it by mastering her energy and putting it to work.

I am blessed to hear such stories of 'lucky synchronicities' among my clients, every day. The formula for making this happen—in other words, Energetic Marketing in a nutshell—goes like this. Firstly, the extraordinary entrepreneur stops looking at business through separation lenses and starts looking at it through energy lenses. 'I am my business and every aspect of it' becomes their motto. They strive to become an embodiment of the business they wish to run.

Secondly, the extraordinary entrepreneur accepts their limitless power; they realise they can create absolutely anything, as long as they are genuinely called to it. Thirdly, they learn to acutely listen to their intuition, and follow it to reap results. Fourthly, they learn to trust the process, because they know that only their soul knows the perfect path to their greatest success. They don't get distracted by the fact that sometimes the journey looks different from what they consciously planned. Once we accept our energetic nature and connect with our clients energetically, we go from chasing clients to attracting clients; we go from hoping for more clients to creating—or, more accurately—giving ourselves more clients. We go from hustling to flow. First things first though: this can only happen from the place of genuine connection and activation of your clients on an energetic level. Yes, effective marketing starts in your mind and heart!

Activation Meditation

Practice this meditation to help you to connect with your ideal clients, as well as anything else you choose to accomplish, on an energetic level. I personally use this meditation practically daily, and credit it for the many miracles happening in my business on a daily basis: for example, potential clients who I planned to contact with a specific offer reaching out to me before I said anything; brand new high-end clients coming to me 'out of nowhere'; opportunities opening up in front of me without conscious action; and money-making and impact-making ideas flooding into my mind with ease.

Of course, our logical mind could argue that these are simply lucky coincidences. And yet, the more you practice energetic selling and marketing, the more certain you become that you can create luck and miracles on demand. I recommend practicing this meditation daily for the best results.

If you wish to download an audio version of this meditation, head to energeticselling.com/resources

1. Close your eyes and direct your attention deep, deep inside your mind; into the centre of your mind. Focus on the single point of your consciousness, like a seed that is so powerful it contains everything that ever was, everything that ever will be, and everything that is. It is a bright white colour, and it is the very centre of you, the single point of energy via which you create everything. Give it a your attention, and acknowledge its power.

2. When you are ready, allow this energy to expand and flood your entire mind. Let it penetrate through every fibre, every cell and every space of your mind. Notice how your mind is becoming activated, your cells are awakening and your mind is awakening. This all-powerful energy—your creative energy—is shifting your mind into the mode of receiving. It cleanses out of your mind whatever doesn't belong there, so you can have clarity, focus, certainty and everything you need for the most effortless creation of that which you choose.

3. When you are ready, let this energy spread further through your throat, cleaning your throat chakra, allowing you to communicate your truth. Allow it to expand into your chest and heart area and the solar plexus, all the way down to the root chakra, activating your inner being. Notice how this all powerful, creative energy—your energy—shifts all the cells in your body. Your entire body awakens. This energy pushes out of your being anything that doesn't belong there, and shifts your vibration right here, right now.

4. Let this energy pulsate. Notice it expanding and contracting, expanding and contracting again. It has its own rhythm. Let it flood throughout the rest of your body, your hands, your feet so your whole body can completely awaken, completely align. Make sure your entire body and mind are bathed in this energy.

5. This is you in your fullness. This is when you stop pretending you are not as powerful as you are. This is when you stop pretending that you don't have all that you choose to be, do, have, right here, right now. This is the real you. Allow yourself to notice all the nuances of your being. What does it feel like to be in your full power? What future memories would you like to create, here and now? Activate inside of you that which you choose to see outside of you. See it, feel it as part of you, as you. Notice what do you see, hear or feel and feel it being you. Embody that future version of you. There is no future, there is no past, there is only now. You are all that you wanted to be, right now. Stay here as long as it is right for you.

6. Allow your energy to spread beyond your physical being. Allow it to expand beyond the room you are in, beyond the city you are in, let it spread across the globe and into the universe. Let it bathe the entire galaxy and let it reach the furthermost corners of the universe. Notice that the whole universe is you. You are the centre of it, and your energy is bathing an entire universe.

7. Notice all those wonderful clients you want to serve. They are part of this holographic universe. They are part of your consciousness. Allow yourself to see or feel them in some way. You may notice them as little stars, or as real people. You may think of someone specific. You may have images coming to your mind. Who is it that you choose to serve? Who are they? They will be a reflection of you and your energy—people in the 'Yes mode' of their lives, committed to their expansion. They are you, after all. See them being activated, perhaps like stars lighting up. Activate more and more of them.

Every time you light them up, pull them energetically towards your physical body, towards your centre; and smile, because you are accepting these reflections of you are for the highest good of all. They are about to become your channel of abundance, and you are about to become their channel of abundance. If there is anyone specific you would love to serve, see them also being lit up. Trust that this thought is reaching their mind and heart. This process is happening between you and every other physical version of your client as we speak, right now. If you choose, you can notice activating many, many, many more soul-clients you are meant to serve, so the law of attraction can bring them to you.

8. Is there anything else you would like to activate in your universe? Anything else you would like to pull towards your physical reality? Whether it is more money, completed successful projects or specific experiences, stay here as long as you need to experience their activation. Don't hold back. Claim what is rightfully yours.

9. Now you are deep in the knowing that you are one with your clients and all else you choose to experience; now you know all of this is inside of you, pause for a moment and ask yourself, 'What is my part in this today?' Is there anything you are inspired to do: an action to take? A way to serve clients? A way to show up? Listen for a few minutes for anything that comes to your mind. What is your part in this? Listen for the ideas that may come to your mind. Open yourself to receive divine inspiration. Simply listen, and take all thoughts and ideas as they are given to you. If no ideas come to your mind, that is okay too. Simply listen. You are practicing connection between you and your higher-self; that part of you that knows all there is to know about the how of embodying the higher version of you who has all you desire. Stay here for a bit.

10. Acknowledge what you have received, or what you didn't receive; that is fine. If you didn't notice any inspiration, trust it will come another time. Acknowledge what you have received and bring that, as well as all those clients, all those activated minds, all that which you want, see that being pulled towards you: your physical you, back to your centre, back inside of you. Acknowledge how rich you are; acknowledge how resourceful you are; acknowledge how powerful you are; and how blessed you are; that all is well, and all that you want is right here, right now. When you are ready, come back into your body fully, open your eyes and start your day as that version of you.

Define your next level soul clients

As you start upgrading your consciousness and start thinking bigger, you may feel inspired to serve on a higher level—whether it is through redesigning and repricing your current offerings, or creating new high-level offerings altogether. With that, of course, often naturally comes the question, 'Who on earth will buy this from me?' For example, it is not uncommon that my clients increase fees for their offerings three, four, even five times for 1-2-1 coaching packages, VIP retreats, group programmes, you name it. Or they create a new service offering, set anywhere between £5K and £50K.

The truth is that, as long as you have a calling to serve on your highest level, and are freaking good at what you do, there will never be a shortage of clients for you—unless you accept otherwise. After all, as we have already established, clients at any level are a reflection of your consciousness and how you choose to experience yourself. So, why would you deny yourself that which is you?

First things first, though: you will want to be crystal clear on who this next level client is: where are they on their journey; what is the most important problem they want to solve; what is their most important desire; and what is preoccupying the majority of their thoughts? Now, I am not talking about your traditional marketing avatar, the demographics of your client (their age, marital and earning status etc.). While it is a good idea to define the demographics of your ideal clients, in marketing your purpose-driven business this tends to have little value. 'Is my client married, single, or in a committed relationship?' for example, has little value beyond relationship coaching, wedding planning and similar professions. If you are a health coach, wondering about your client's relationship status can lead to confusion more than anything else.

My typical marketing avatar, for example, is a woman coach, aged 35-55, in a committed relationship or married. Having said that, I have trained and coached women who are in the 20s or 60s age groups; I have worked with men and with non-coaches, and I have worked with plenty of single women and jetsetters. When it comes to demographics, I say it as it is: I don't give a damn that much. Naturally, in my marketing I talk to coaches—because I am one—and I often use examples from my family life. I also have a rather strong accent. As a result, I tend to attract plenty of mothers who want to grow their purpose-driven business, and women from all over the world who resonate with my 'she moved countries and succeeded' story.

In other words, I tend to attract clients similar to me. This, in purpose-driven businesses, is a very natural process. Those clients who resonate with your personality are a match to your energy, and see great value in your work. They will buy from you, no matter what their demographics. What you want to be damn clear about, though, is how your perfect-for-you client thinks. You want to be sure of their personal characteristics, their qualities, and what is their 'Oh shit!' point: this is the moment when they are ready to commit and buy. We will talk about that more in the next chapter. Because it is only when you have this clarity that you can set a strong intention to attract these clients, to serve these clients; and you can adjust your marketing, energetically and practically, to become fully booked with these exact clients.

EXTRAORDINARY GROWTH CHALLENGE: FIVE STAR SOUL CLIENT POLICY

TAKE TIME TO DEFINE the perfect-for-you client who will allow you to do your best work, serve at your highest level, and have a freaking good time while doing so. This is the type of client who will energise you when you work with them, rather than drain you. These are the clients who will benefit from your service most, and who will become your brand ambassadors, recommending many other clients to you.

Who are they? Grab a piece of paper and divide it into two columns. In the first column, write down all the qualities of the clients that you will not accept when you recognise them. An example might be as follows:

My five star soul-client will not:
• Have a victim mentality (operate from To Me Consciousness by default)
• Pay late or be a non-payer
• Be closed to constructive feedback
• Be dishonest with me or other people
• Cancel sessions or show up late for appointments
• Make constant excuses as to why they didn't follow up on their commitments to themselves

Don't hold back. Make a comprehensive list of potential qualities that may make your work less enjoyable, or jeopardise your client's results.

In the second column, write down the opposite of the qualities you defined in the first column. Examples might include the following.

My five star soul client will:
• Have a great deal of personal responsibility
• Always pay on time
• Be highly coachable and open to constructive feedback
• Be honest with me and everyone else
• Always show up on time, except for very rare emergencies
• Follow up on their commitments

Again, make this list very comprehensive. Add to it if needed. This is a blueprint of your soul-aligned client and the type of people who will not only make your work extremely successful and enjoyable, but also are the people who will be channels to the extraordinary growth in your business that you wish to create.

'If you wish to serve at your highest level,
you have to become your highest level.'

Let me share with you something personal: a little
embarrassing, but very relevant. With the birth of my third
boy, I found myself holding plenty of excessive baby
weight. I expected it to drop off naturally, as it had with my
first two boys; but unfortunately it didn't happen this time.
Because of my bulimic past, I am not a fan of diets —and
frankly, I really like my food—so I decided to exercise it off
instead. Plus, it was not that I hated myself being a little
bigger, I simply prefer being slimmer, and that is where my
choosing and desire ends. I decided to hire a personal
trainer for three sessions per week. She came to my house
and tortured me real good! I felt great about introducing
more exercise into my week, except that from time to time
I had more important things to do, and I simply cancelled
my personal trainer. I kid you not: every time I did that,
someone cancelled with me in my business, typically a
scheduled sales call. It came to the point where I had to
acknowledge to myself: 'I had better start committing to
myself fully, otherwise how can I expect my clients to
commit to themselves?'

You see, the behaviour of our clients—potential and
existing ones—can only reflect back at us that which is
happening inside of ourselves. So, if you want to attract your
next soul-aligned clients with ease, it is essential that you
become a perfect match to them in the first place.

I'll give you another example of how this works. Some
time ago, Lydia, an intuitive coach for women entrepreneurs,
came to me sharing about not getting the results she wanted
from her marketing and selling. She was doing everything by
the book; she had years of coaching experience under her

belt; and yet every month she ended up with only enough money to pay her bills and sustain her current lifestyle. She wanted more, a lot more. On further questioning, it became obvious to me that what we needed to work on was tweaking her energetic blueprint. It made a lot of sense to her, and she was eager to start working with me.

The only problem was Lydia didn't have enough money for the deposit, yet alone the full coaching fee, which was multi-five-figure. 'I'm waiting for clients to pay my invoices, and when they do, I will come back and pay the deposit.' That wording caught my attention. I asked Lydia to tell me more about waiting for her clients to take action. 'Does it happen to you often, waiting for other people to take action?' 'All the time!' Lydia replied. She was experiencing a pattern in her business, waiting for other people to take action, which was clearly not working in her favour.

I explained how her clients were mirroring her internal pattern and how it was up to her to break it. 'What is one action you can take today to break the waiting pattern? How can you move forward without waiting?' On consideration, Lydia replied, 'If you allow me to, I can pay a smaller deposit today and pay the rest within two weeks. I will go out there and make it happen, but I would like to commit today.' I accepted this arrangement, and within two weeks Lydia had made enough money to pay the full deposit for the coaching, largely because all those clients she was waiting for were—amazingly—taking action and getting back to her one by one. We started coaching together, working on Lydia's energetic blueprint, namely: removing the programming about money; going from passive selling to active selling; and adopting new ways of thinking when it comes to selling and marketing. Lydia created nothing short of extraordinary growth in her business. In the following month, she increased her average monthly sales revenue by ten times, an increase she was able to sustain for the months to come. She took her business to an entirely new level in one swoop, and that process started by her willingness to break unhelpful patterns within her first conversation with me.

The exercise above, The Five Star Soul Client Policy, will be very handy when you decide to do that too: to break unhelpful patterns in your business and become a perfect match to your next-level client. Here is what you need to do next. Review the left column of your five star client policy and ask yourself, 'Am I practicing any of these qualities in any area of my life?' For example, if you expect your ideal next-level clients to pay on time, every time, you had better make sure you practice the same: and not only in regards to your business responsibilities, but also in relation to your household bills and financial responsibilities in every area of your life. If you notice any gaps or opportunities for improvement on your part, set a plan and make commitments to eliminate this pattern from your life. Review the entire list of qualities you won't accept in your next level clients, and make sure you have a plan for not embodying these qualities anywhere in your life.

Then, move onto column two of the five star client exercise and ask yourself, 'Am I this woman, in every area of my life? If not, what am I going to do about it?' For example, if one of the expectations of your clients is: 'They always follow up on their commitments to themselves', then make sure you do exactly the same: again, not only in business but in every other area of your life. Set a plan for how you are going to do that.

This exercise can be a hard pill to swallow. It may challenge you. It may leave you feeling, 'Bloody hell, do I really need to do this?' But it is probably one of the most important things you can do for yourself and your business. It is exactly these kinds of changes that will make you a far more resourceful and powerful woman and position you to be able to attract your high-end clients with ease.

Here is another reason for attending to your five star client policy and putting an action plan in place for becoming a perfect reflection of the client you wish to serve.

Give yourself a gift of time, and do the exercise in fullness. Make an action plan of things to adjust in your behaviour, your patterns and your life, that may currently be unfavourably reflecting back at you in your business, or simply stopping you from experiencing your greatest success. It is the only way to put your energetic selling and marketing fully to work. And it is incredibly rewarding.

IN THIS CHAPTER YOU HAVE DISCOVERED

• You are already connected to your clients, but it is important to do the process of connecting.

• Your clients are a reflection of your consciousness.

• No matter at what level you decide to serve your clients, there are always plenty of clients who will benefit hugely from your work and gladly pay for your services unless you accept otherwise.

• Any unhelpful pattern in your business is a reflection of patterns you practice yourself. If you want to change it, you need to change yourself in the first place.

• To attract next level clients with ease, you need to become their mirror reflection in the first place. A Five Star Soul Client Policy will help you with that.

Before we move onto the next chapter, ask yourself these questions.

1. What pattern in my business do I wish to break? How am I going to do that?
2. Do I approach my marketing through the idea of separation, or unity? Does this approach serve me? Is there anything I desire to change?
3. To what extend am I willing to become a perfect mirror to the clients I choose to serve?

In the next chapter, we will go deeper into the 'how' of connecting with your clients on the emotional and energetic level, so your marketing can become a lot more fruitful!

6
Connection

Transcend All Business Limitations

'Action-based marketing is limited to tactics and strategies. Energetic marketing transcends all limitations and enables you to attract perfect-for-you clients with ease. '

'FEEL FREE TO STAY in one of my apartments!' proclaimed Donald, after I shared with him that I was filming for a day in Canary Wharf, London. What a nice gesture, I thought: so lovely that I couldn't refuse, and a great reason to catch up with Donald after more than a decade of silence. He had worked for me, while I was running one of the McDonald's stores: a young guy from Zimbabwe who worked extremely hard to support his family back home. He had earned respect among his colleagues and managers alike.

Later that week, after we wrapped up the day of filming, Donald, myself, and a few of my employees went for a drink in a Sky Bar in his apartment block. The view overlooking London was heavenly, and it was a perfect place to talk for hours. I learned that Donald had moved on a long way from flipping burgers and mopping the floors in McDonald's.

Now, he owned several apartments in central London, and several successful companies; he enthusiastically shared with me his plans to build a school back in his home country. Then he suddenly said, 'I have got to tell you Lenka, my success all started with you.' Noticing the confused look on my face, he explained. 'You were the first person in my life who truly believed in me. I took that belief, and applied it in business.'

What he said gave me goosebumps, and re-affirmed what I had come to believe long ago: that there is tremendous power in viewing other people from the perspective of their highest potential. In this chapter, you will see how we are constantly projecting our beliefs onto our existing and potential clients; and how they cannot do anything else but respond to our projection.

Another example of this aspect, from a few years ago, was a mother of an eight-year-old girl who attended my NLP Coach Training. She expressed her concerns about her daughter, who took little interest in doing her homework, struggled to keep up with the school curriculum and 'no matter how much I tell her homework is important and she can't be lazy, she will not listen.' 'Is that what you tell her?', I asked, 'that she is lazy?' 'Well, she is lazy, and it worries me,' was her answer; then added, 'However now, having completed your course, I understand the change needs to come from me in the first place.'

As a result, this mom changed the way she thought and communicated with her daughter. She went out of her way to acknowledge her daughter every time she completed something or did something well: when she made her bed; when she helped her sibling; when she cleaned the plates after a dinner; and when she crafted or drew a lovely picture. 'I love how focused/diligent/smart you are,' were the words she learned to use. Several months later, she reported back to me how a significant change in her daughter had taken place. 'We no longer need to talk her into doing her homework or completing school projects. She simply does it, and does it the best she can. Also, she has dramatically changed her behaviour at home. This change wasn't sudden but rather gradual, but it is an incredible change indeed,' she concluded.

How is this relevant to growing your business? You see, each person in your audience is like that daughter. They can show up in a million different ways; they have that flexibility. The way they show up depends on what they think of themselves and that is, in turn, often influenced by what other people think of them. You are one of those people and it is your responsibility as an extraordinary marketer and change-maker, to inspire your clients to show up in the most powerful way. You are influencing the way they behave through what you believe about them; so you might as well do it consciously.

You see, this very moment you are projecting your own beliefs onto your potential and your existing clients, as well as onto your team members, suppliers and so forth. You project your beliefs about what they are or aren't capable of; how creative or limited they are; and how powerful or powerless they are. These beliefs are being reflected back at you through your clients, often without you even knowing about it.

Dina Behrman, an owner of a Public Relations agency, brought a challenge into one of our business coaching sessions. She had launched a new online course for entrepreneurs who wanted to learn how to harness the power of PR themselves, rather than hire a specialist. Her goal was to serve 40 entrepreneurs in the first round of the course and yet, only two days before the closing date, only four people had signed up. Dina said, 'My email opening rate is very low, and people are not responding to my offer.' Together, we reviewed the offer, sales page, email headings and Dina's marketing. We tweaked only a few things, but there was nothing that would make or break Dina's launch. She is a smart cookie and a great marketer. I told her: 'Darling, it's time to tweak your energy too. It is time to see your audience for who you want them to be.'

We checked two additional aspects of her business. First, was Dina mirroring the behaviour of her clients in some way? For example, was she ignorant about important information in her business or life? Was she not taking meaningful actions aligned with her growth? As per the previous chapter, we made sure she was mirroring the client she wanted to serve. It turned out there wasn't misalignment in her mirroring, so we proceeded to check the second factor, which is lurking often behind consistent, technically correct, yet ineffective marketing: limiting projection onto her clients.

Dina had developed an unhelpful set of beliefs about her potential clients: that they were ignoring her messages; that they didn't see the value in her offering, certainly not enough to take action and pay for the course; and that they didn't engage with her content. I gave Dina a series of focused exercises to complete in her own time: to write down 20+ ways her clients would benefit from the Public Relations course; 20+ reasons her clients could find ways to pay for the course, even when they had financial challenges; and 20+ reasons her clients loved reading her emails and other online content, and responding to her call to action. Through simple exercises such as these, Dina was able to challenge her beliefs about her clients and consciously choose what she wanted to project onto them. Incredibly, within the next 48 hours, Dina made 37 sales for her new course. 'My email open-rate went up significantly, and I couldn't quite believe how easy it was to turn this situation around, by completing a couple of mindset exercises,' Dina shared with me excitedly.

The formula for greater success with your marketing and selling efforts is actually simple. If you don't like the way your clients behave, first, check whether you need to change your own attitudes and behaviours, so your clients can reflect back at you differently. Then, change how you view your clients. Over time and often immediately, they will adjust their behaviour to reflect your new projection.

Time to put this formula into action!

EXTRAORDINARY GROWTH CHALLENGE: CHOOSE HOW YOU VIEW YOUR CLIENTS

IN THE LAST CHAPTER, we talked about the importance of reviewing unhelpful behaviour patterns in your business and changing yourself in order to break these patterns and mirror your dream clients. This chapter and the following exercise will build on this principle, and is designed to help you realise what you are projecting onto your existing and potential clients. It will help you change your limiting beliefs about them, so they can start reflecting back to you differently.

Step One

Ask yourself, 'What do I believe about my clients? What do I say to myself about my clients behaviours when I am selling and marketing?' Pay particular attention to your negative assumptions and generalisations. Here are a few examples.

- 'I attract people who cannot afford my services.'
- 'People in my audience like and comment on my stuff, but they don't buy. They don't consider it important.'
- 'They are not ready to step up.'
- 'People don't engage with my content.'

Step Two

Once you have a comprehensive list of your own unhelpful projections about your clients, take each one and write down 20 or more reasons why the opposite may be true. For example, if one of your assumptions is that you attract clients who cannot afford your services, write down 20 or more reasons why they will be able to afford your services. There are several examples below.

- My clients are infinitely resourceful. When something is important to them, they will find a way to make it happen.
- My clients are powerful adults who can see when something is so valuable that they cannot afford not to invest in it.
- My services help my clients in such-and-such a way. This is more than a good reason for my clients to stop saying to themselves, 'I can't afford it' and start asking themselves, 'How can I make this happen?'

Writing down 20 or more reasons why the opposite of your unhelpful assumption about your clients is true may stretch you. You may feel that you are 'making things up'. And you know what? That is okay.

Completing this exercise will do three things for you and your business. Firstly, your personal energy—your default attraction point—will shift and you will change what you project onto your clients, hence opening the channel of abundance that was not there before. Secondly, you will gain new, inspired ideas for marketing and selling your services more effectively. Among your 20 reasons you may find several great ideas for sales letters, social media posts, webinars and so on; they will be new ideas that will talk to your client's minds and hearts. Thirdly, this shift in your energy will also inform the way you sell and market to your clients in the future. You will stop unconsciously saving people and instead, you will start empowering them; a simple but significant change that itself has the power to completely transform the way you communicate; and ultimately, transform your business results.

Are you saving or empowering your clients?

I recall my client Sam complaining to me. 'I currently serve five high-end clients, half the amount of clients I would like to serve at any one time, and yet I already feel exhausted. It makes me wonder how else can I grow my business.' There is no point in developing new business growth strategies if the fundamentals are not right, and it was clear to me from Sam's language that there were a few things needing urgent attention.

It turned out that Sam made lots of exceptions 'to meet her clients' needs'. She agreed to delayed payment plans that remained long after the coaching relationship was completed because, as she said, 'Some clients could not afford the monthly fee.' And of course, some clients didn't honour that commitment either. She was on her email numerous times a day answering her client's questions and helping them fix their problems. She often coached in the late hours of the day, because some of her clients 'couldn't make it during normal coaching hours'. In addition, she typically gave her clients extra coaching sessions, especially when they didn't make changes as quickly and easily as they wanted.

Furthermore, this 'saving' mentality filtered through in her marketing. She used phrases such as, 'I know it can be tricky to put money together for this course, so I created a long-term payment plan for people who cannot afford it right now' or 'I will be on the call for you 24/7, so whenever you have any challenge, I will be there for you.' It was no surprise that Sam was feeling exhausted! She had an unconscious need to save her clients rather than empower them: an attitude that many service providers—myself included at times—can accidentally fall into. It is an attitude, which once you adopt it, can filter through to every aspect of your business; and it doesn't help, but hurts both your clients and your business.

When you market to your audience from the attitude of saving, you are probably making it incredibly easy for them to invest in your service. While this can increase your sales short-term, it can cause many problems down the line. As an extraordinary entrepreneur and changemaker, you don't only want to serve people. You want to serve the right people and it is certainly not going to happen by wanting to save others. It is the way to train your clients to be lazy in their thinking and stay in To Me Consciousness. They can, since you'll fix all of their problems! You can soon become tired, resentful and helping your clients to get results can become a chore. If your calling is to scale your impact many fold, choose empowering your clients instead of saving them and do so from the moment they get to know about you through your marketing, through to delivering your service. That is the only way to grow your business with ease and for your clients to benefit from your services to the max and gain phenomenal results.

Strong boundaries are a must!

You see: like us, our potential and existing clients have two selves at work; their ego or lower-self and their higher-self.

> *'The most effective marketing and selling happens in the form of acknowledgement of your clients' ego-self and inspiring them to step into their higher-self.'*

Notice, I didn't say 'buying into ego-self', 'believing your client's ego-self', or 'pandering to their ego-self'. Acknowledgement of your client's ego-self is very important, but going beyond that it is unhelpful, for both your clients and your business. It is being aware of this fine line that will help you to engage with your client's hearts and minds, and make your marketing efforts incredibly fruitful.

There are five principles to make this concept work for your marketing.

1. Lead your marketing and selling materials not with your potential clients' problems, but rather, how these problems translate into your clients' internal self-talk and real life situations.

For example, the problem your clients may face is a lack of clients. By all means, you could talk to your clients about how you can help them to attract more clients through your SEO services, marketing websites, coaching, or whatever service you provide. That type of marketing will capture your clients' minds. However, your clients buy with their hearts. It is our feelings that trigger logical reasoning when it comes to making buying decisions and to engage your client's emotions in your marketing you want to talk about what is happening as a result of their problem. For example, the lack of clients in their lives and how their service will help change that situation.

As a result of the lack of the clients, the person you market to may have divorce papers on the table, because her husband is telling her every day how selfish she is to focus on her business, instead of getting a real job. Her ego-thoughts might be saying, 'Maybe, I am not cut out for this' and yet, the idea of giving up on her dream of running a successful business is unacceptable; too hurtful. Or perhaps she is beating herself up because her children are getting older and she is aware she cannot provide them with what is best for them. She desperately wants to be a good example to them and yet she doesn't know 'how to make this stupid business work'. These are factors your clients will truly worry about; and the lack of clients is only the surface problem. So, talk to them about that! Let them clearly know what the real problem is and how your service will help them to change these situations.

2. Never be afraid to be vulnerable and show your clients a little piece of your your heart and mind.

If you experience any of the client's deep problems—the type of problems that can keep them up at night—be brave and open up about it. Share with your clients what happened to you and how you overcame your challenge. While vulnerability on demand is not attractive and can come across as a 'sob story', genuinely sharing with your audience how you dealt with—or are dealing with—real life challenges, can build a huge amount of trust and heart-to-heart connection. Below is a personal example. I wrote it and shared it online in several entrepreneurial groups where my soul-aligned clients gather, at the beginning of my online coaching business. I remember trembling before pressing the 'publish' button. I was afraid I would lose credibility as a coach; afraid that people would not take me seriously anymore; and afraid that I wouldn't come across as professional. My ego was having a field day! Yet, because I felt inspired to help through my sharing with other people, I published it anyway. What happened next? Hundreds upon hundreds of women entrepreneurs resonated with my story so much that they researched me online and joined my community. Remarkable! Naturally, this led to a good few high-end coaching clients, giving my business a healthy boost. This was one of the first times I learned about the value of overcoming our own ego—exactly when we want to be professional and credible—and open our heart from time to time to vulnerably; and I have never regretted it.

Here is that personal example of my vulnerability from a few years back, which I know will help you. I had a calling to expand on my 1-2-1 coaching and offline training courses, and to create a life-changing online coaching programme. This gave birth to my Get Fully Booked programme. And a couple of months later, I started to gather the materials, outlined everything and started the initial preparations for the programme. I set my mind to launching the programme in the next month. But then a bombshell landed; I learned that my colleague Becky, who was a well-established coach in the market was launching another round of her amazing programmes in at the same time and similar to mine. But hers was cheaper. My heart sank, and the whole comparison game started. For a good few days, I put everything on pause. Why? Because of the voices in my head, the doubters: 'Who am I to do this?' 'Why would anyone want to sign up for my programme when they can sign up with Becky?' And then there is Marie Forleo and her amazing *B-School*, and Kimra Luna and her famous *Be True, Brand You* course!'

I basically went through the list of all the women I admired and why they and their programmes were so much better than mine. Well, you probably understand the point here. This kind of thinking doesn't work. Instead, I had to remind myself of all the reasons why I had been following my calling since I started my business eight years ago and why I have every right to follow it now. I had to remind myself why I was different and attracting different women out of seven billion people on this planet. I had to remind myself of all the reasons why I am worthy to do this, how I am putting my all into it and why, by making myself small, I am taking away the opportunity from women out there who are meant to be part of my programme. So, I let go, I by-passed the saboteurs and guess what? The natural flow began.

The door to my programme was not yet open, but I had ten amazing women signed up for it already. I also reached out to other amazing experts in their respective industries and they all said a whole-hearted 'Yes' to contribute expert content to my programme. I felt so humbled! I was overwhelmed with support and help to spread awareness about my programme and I felt sure again; and excited; and blessed; and connected to the knowledge that we all have our unique purpose and place on this big wide planet. This goes for you too; yes, YOU. Becky is amazing because she is Becky and gives Becky to the world. Marie gives Marie. Kimra gives Kimra. You give you. That is how we will change the world: together.

The lesson to remember is that once you establish a heart-to-heart connection with your clients, they will be much more likely to respond to your Call to Action, even if it is only a few hours, days, or weeks later. By the way, since its humble inception the *Get Fully Booked* programme has helped hundreds of entrepreneurs to start and grow successful online coaching and purpose-driven businesses. Later, it became a part of my Extraordinary Growth Academy for women entrepreneurs who want to create extraordinary impact in the world.

3. Exude certainty when creating a bridge between your client's problem and solution.

Investing in high-end services requires your buyers to consider this question: 'will this work?' Only when we are certain the answer is a loud 'Yes' for us, are we willing to invest in solving our problems. Help your clients to have that certainty by being certain yourself. If you haven't done so yet, be clear on what exactly is a return on your clients' investment in your services and how much it is worth to them: financially; emotionally; spiritually; and physically. Then, communicate this attitude with confidence in your marketing. For example, replace, 'This course will help you learn about effective presenting skills' with 'This course will turn you into a charismatic speaker and unlock the power of your message to impact millions of other people.' People won't pay high-end fees to simply learn. They can Google a few words to find all the information they are looking for. They want results. Help them to be certain that as long as they do their part, they can achieve the results and transformations they are looking for.

4. Embody the energy of the business you wish to run and let your marketing show it.

I recall a conversation with one of my clients during our first session together. I asked her, 'Once you grow your business to the level you want and you imagine yourself running it day to day, what do you feel? What is the most prevailing emotion when you think of that?' She answered, 'Accomplishment. I would feel very accomplished'. I continued, 'Good and when you think of your business today and the day to day running of it, what is the underlying emotion?' She replied without hesitation, 'Struggle'. I asked her next, 'Can you see the disconnect? With your marketing and selling, you are probably doing your best to communicate the power of your work, and how your clients will feel when they invest in your services. And yet you are doing so from the energy of struggle. That can't work in your favour, because your clients don't respond to words or marketing and selling tactics alone. They pick up on your energy along the way, the very thing that informs the words and strategies you use.'

We explored her personal activities and experiences, which naturally gave her the sense of accomplishment she was looking for in her business. I learned that she loved running, but doesn't do it as often as she wanted because marketing and growing her business took priority. That was about to change and very rapidly. When this client understood she had to give herself permission to embody the energy of the business she wished to run so her clients could feel it channelled into her marketing and sales process, did she start to hit the running track daily guilt-free, and learned to show that side of herself in her business. Only a few days later, she reported back to me that she had, 'never experienced the level of client engagement she now has' and her marketing started to bear more fruit very quickly.

How about you, gorgeous? What choices can you make that will help you to embody the energy of what you offer? Allow yourself to do it and use this side of yourself in your marketing. Your clients will feel your essence; the very thing they are buying when they invest in your services.

5. Develop trust by establishing yourself as an expert.

We women entrepreneurs are—generally speaking— chronically shy to communicate our brilliance to the world. We don't want to toot our own horn. We don't want to come across as bragging. If this is you, listen up, gorgeous. You must stop listening to the, 'I don't want to come across this way or that way' voice in your head. Instead, simply let your audience know—unashamedly—what you are about. Because it is simply not enough for you to know that you are an incredibly skilled coach/changemaker/service provider, etc. Your potential clients must know it too otherwise there is a gap in perception that can potentially cost you a fortune. It is your responsibility to fill that gap and align your perception of yourself as an expert in your field and your market's perception of you.

I recall a talk by Rob Brown, bestselling author of *Build Your Reputation* and creator of the Business Development Academy. Rob jump-started his own extraordinary growth by claiming his place as the No. 1 expert in reputation building for entrepreneurs in the United Kingdom. 'Who can disapprove that?' he said to himself. He simply claimed that place, marketed it and sold from that perspective. The word got around fast. Rob was invited to many stages where he shared his story of taking responsibility for your reputation and his business grew rapidly as a result.

You don't need the level of Rob's confidence to call yourself the No. 1 expert in the world or your country. Only 10% of it will do. It is simply about becoming clear on your place in the marketplace, your zone of genius and communicating this clearly to your audience.

Putting it all together

Dr Kavetha Sun, MD, a Harvard trained psychiatrist and Infidelity Expert, has a knack for using these principles in her marketing. Here is an example of her Facebook advertising.

'I can't believe he cheated on me, my life is shattered. I don't know if I should stay or leave.' I get it. Being cheated on is the one of the worst things a human being can experience. It is a sucker punch to the gut. And it turns our world upside down. The obsession to unearth every single thing about the affair becomes all-consuming. Couple this with the daily emotional roller coaster, and not being able to sleep most nights, and it almost seems easier to just pull the plug, right?? Hit the 'escape' button and restart everything. But then again, what about all those years of love, memories of travelling, building your home, raising your babies together, those times that he stood by you, was it all a lie? Should you throw all that away?

Believe me, I know how paralyzing these questions can be. When I was in this terrible spot several years ago, I instinctively wanted to reach for anything that would give me my dignity back, some way to make sure no one could ever hurt me this way again and pulling the plug felt like the only option. I have since learned a lot through my training as a psychiatrist at Harvard and as a couple's therapist. My practice is focused solely on helping couples through the crisis of infidelity. This is what I do every day and I love my job. Sadly, when couples come to me, I often see hurt partners contemplating divorce based on myths, rather than facts. Just like I had all those years ago.

Now, I am not saying every marriage should be saved. Not at all, I myself have counselled couples to call it quits, because after a thorough evaluation, it was clearly the best option for everyone involved. But given that divorce is a long, painful, expensive ordeal that often leaves people emotionally and financially depleted, I want you to intentionally choose your decision, rather than react impulsively in a haze of pain and anger because when we make drastic decisions based on myths, it is like jumping from the frying pan into the fire. I have complied all you need to know about these myths in my free ebook, *The Top Five Myths About infidelity*; and *How to Decide if You Should Stay or Leave.*

Your marriage might have a chance of complete healing. Even if you think he is in love with the other person and even if you have called the attorney. When you understand the truth behind these myths, you can figure out if you should stay and give your marriage a chance to heal and become more intimate and honest than before—yes, this is possible—or if it really is too late. My mission is to help save marriages that are worth saving. Is yours worth saving? Let's find out. See you on the inside.'

Notice the six logical steps that Dr Kavetha Sun went through progressively, in her marketing piece. She takes her readers with her on a journey and converts them to potentially being her clients by the end of the advertisement because she connected with their hearts and minds and gave them what they want to take their pain away.

- How she started her advert with the reader's deep problems: what is happening in their lives and in their hearts and minds.
- How she built trust with her readers: opening up about her own experience with infidelity in the past and showing her own vulnerability.
- How she effortlessly established her credibility: mentioning Harvard University and what she does now in her business.
- How she inspired her reader to step into their higher self: seek alternative solutions to their problems.
- How she stimulated hope: by connecting with the emotions of the reader.
- How she exuded certainty of a positive outcome: making the right decision, which builds the reader's trust in her ability to help them achieve this same wonderful result for themselves.

Bingo! Many people who read this advertisement contact Dr Kavetha Sun and become her clients, because they want to achieve exactly what she is offering and she connected with their hearts and minds with a few simple words. Dr Kavetha Sun is not only excellent at what she does but she is also great at communicating her expertise to the market of her potential clients.

And now it is time to outline how you too, can use these principles in your marketing. Your business will thank you for it.

IN THIS CHAPTER YOU HAVE DISCOVERED

• When you want to attract the right clients to you—clients who will engage with you and love to invest in your services—you will need to:

1. Mirror your perfect client.
2. Project your beliefs onto your clients consciously, rather than unconsciously.
3. Talk to your ideal clients' minds and hearts.

• There is a huge power in holding your clients in the highest regard.
• Empowering people is far more powerful than marketing and serving from the unconscious need to save people.
• The key to effective marketing is to acknowledge your clients' ego-self while inspiring them to step into their higher-self.
• Our emotions are largely responsible for making buying decisions. It is our responsibility as change-makers, to not only engage our clients' minds, but also their hearts.

Before we move on to the next chapter, here are three questions you must ask yourself:

1. What will your client feel once they invest in your services and they achieve the results and transformation they want?
2. How can you embody this emotion?
3. How can you exude this emotion in your marketing?

In the next chapter, you will commit to one thing that has the potential to change everything in your business and set you on a path of continual, extraordinary growth. It is time to fall in love with selling!

7
ENERGETIC SELLING

THE PATH TO YOUR EXTRAORDINARY GROWTH

*'Committing to selling is committing to
expressing your soul at the highest level.'*

'GOODBYE MY DARLINGS! Have a wonderful day!' I kissed and hugged my two boys as they disappeared into their classrooms. It was a day like any other. On my way home I stopped at the local shopping centre to stock up our groceries. I didn't have any cash on me, nor was I sure how much money I actually had on my debit card. I decided to check. But what stared at me from the cash machine was only £7.30! You might as well have shown me a giant tarantula wearing pink socks on each of its eight legs. I didn't know whether to freeze in shock, laugh out loud, prepare to fight, or all of those actions at once. 'Bloody hell. Are you serious?' I said to the machine, as if it was going to show me a different number, which of course it wasn't.

There I was, thinking how the hell did I get here; flashes of various moments of my life appeared in front of me: the moment when I sold my house more than six years ago to finance my studies and start up my own business as an

121

accredited trainer and coach. The moment when I was swapping a company BMW for a £100 paid-in-cash Polo, which had seen better days, because surely a car was only a small and temporary sacrifice on my way to becoming a successful entrepreneur who was going to change many peoples' lives. The moment when I was parking this same car two blocks away from my meetings with new potential clients and walking the rest of the way on foot, because someone might see me driving that car! Then, the moment when I bought my own BMW 5 Series, with a beige leather interior a few years later, because my business was making enough money to afford it. The moment when my second son was born in a small apartment I called my home at the time, and having to leave him with my husband at home only a few days later because I had a training course to deliver, yep, you get the picture; I was that committed to my work. The moment when we went on our first luxury family holiday because, yay, I could finally afford that too! The moment when my six figure business, which I loved so much was 'stolen away from me'—or that is how I felt at the time—and I had to start all over again...back to networking locally, from morning until evening, working my butt off every waking hour of the day; back to checking the prices of tomatoes before—of course—buying the cheapest ones available. Only this time, I could say, 'I used to run a successful business I loved.' Not that it was worth anything anymore!

Now, here I was experiencing possibly the most embarrassing moment in my life, with that £7.30 laughing maliciously in my face. Six years of working on making my business successful and this is where I had arrived? Not being able to afford a family dinner, struggling to pay the basic household bills each month, unless at least a couple of kind people book me as their coach? I was in shock! Little did I know that this hugely embarrassing moment was to become one of the most defining moments of my life.

I didn't walk home that day, I ran. Once I closed the front door, I caught my breath, made myself a cup of coffee and opened the box with every business card I had collected during the previous 18 months, and I started calling. If anyone had vaguely expressed an interest in working with me, and they were not yet my client, they received a call. If anyone had praised my work, they got a call. And I said to each and every one of those people, 'I can help you solve such-and-such problem; would you be interested to hear about it?' It was awkward. It was uncomfortable.

I was waffling half the time. But by the end of that day, I had sold services worth £1,800. Okay, not exactly the ready stash for buying a new Porsche; but you know what? I knew deep down that everything was changing that day and change it did! Since then, I have never had to check the prices of tomatoes again. I attracted coaching clients with more and more ease, eventually serving clients from more than thirty countries around the world and often with a client waiting list. I was finally living a dream I had held onto for so long—doing something I deeply love—being generously paid for it, and having my heart filled with purpose. One of the biggest reasons for this happening was because I had finally committed to selling every one of my working days. I learned to make selling my priority. But it could not happen without changing my perspective about what selling is and what it is not. And that is the purpose of this chapter, my darling! When you are not selling your genius daily, or you want to do something else rather than sell, it is time to change. It is time to change your relationship with selling, fall in love with it and commit to making it your daily priority.

That is the only way you can increase your impact, and be generously paid for doing your best work in the world.

Are you selling or avoiding?

Here is an interesting point. Until that 'oh-dear-I-only-have-£7.30-left moment' in my life, I thought I was doing everything I needed to do to grow my business. I attended a million-and-one local networking events. I grabbed every free speaking opportunity I could. I posted on my Facebook page regularly. I sent out regular newsletters to my tiny mailing list. I was sharing with other people exactly how hard I was working on growing my business and yet, I kept complaining to my friends that I don't see the fruits of my hard work as much as I wanted. The only reason was that while I was doing everything and anything that was easy for me, I avoided selling like the plague. I was saying to myself, 'But I can't be following up on people again and again. I have more integrity than that. If they really want to work with me, they will get back to me. I really don't want to come across as salesy or pushy. That is not who I am!'

That was my logic, and my excuse to avoid selling. All the while, I was crying my eyes out because no matter what I did, my business was not growing! As it turned out, I wasn't the only one who thought the business would magically grow without selling. Some time ago, I ran an online poll, asking women entrepreneurs and change-makers, 'Honestly speaking, are you selling as often as it is needed to grow your business the way you want?' Incredibly, more than 80% of the poll responders answered, No. The results of this informal poll may be surprising. According to a Gong.io analysis of more than 30,000 B2B sales calls, women close sales deals 11% higher than men. It is clear to everyone that women have great sales skills.

Something changes, however, when women decide to go it alone. Selling is no longer about selling their employer's product. We start to associate ourselves with whatever we sell; we behave as if we were not selling our product or service, but rather ourselves, which is not natural for most women. I have heard time and time again from women who previously excelled at selling in the corporate environment how challenging they find selling their services once they set up their own business. What they all say is, 'I don't like pushing people to buy! I don't want to come across as desperate!' There may be a multitude of reasons for us, women entrepreneurs, not selling our services adequately. But when all is said and done, there is only one reason for it; we consider selling to be something that it is not. We often associate selling with our past experiences, when we have been on the receiving end of questionable selling techniques. These unfortunate experiences can lead to an assumption that there isn't a way to sell and keep one's full integrity, so we often put selling on the back seat of our business.

> *'Change what you believe about selling and
> your sale results will change.'*

It is time to overhaul your sales beliefs. Let's have a look at your thinking patterns and assumptions that may be quietly working in the background of your mind, discouraging you from the most important activity in your businesses. These beliefs may be affecting your personal energy field and can be hindering your ability to grow your business with ease. Let's address them once and for all, so you can fall in love with selling and commit to it fully! Each of the following five quotations are genuine responses from my online survey and I address each in turn to help you revamp your mindset and commit to successful selling.

1. 'I don't want to come across as salesy or pushy.'

This is probably the number one fear for women change-makers. While it is understandable, it is worthwhile realising that any type of, 'I don't want to come across this way or that way,' is ego-self thinking. It is only our ego that cares about how we come across in front of other people. Once you step into Through Me, or As Me, Consciousness you realise that any fear of criticism or judgement is simply a fear of self-judgement. What is the easiest way to overcome this unhelpful way of thinking? Clinical psychologists suggest that people suffering from social anxiety need to redirect their attention away from themselves to another person. It is one of the most effective ways to become less anxious and with practice, confident in social interactions.

The same point applies to selling. You cannot feel nervous about it when you direct your attention fully onto the client who may benefit from your service. Put aside all your needs and your thoughts about how you come across or don't come across when you talk to people about what you offer. Make them the centre of the universe in that moment. Be curious. Be honest. Notice how your energy shifts when you do so. Your higher-self loves to sell; sure, she probably doesn't call it selling, but for sure she is excited about giving people the opportunity to transform, to grow and to honour themselves. Once you direct your focus onto your clients and sell as your higher-self, it is possible that the ego-self thoughts will still cross your mind from time to time. Perhaps a thought will disturb you, such as, 'I can't possibly say this because my client will think I am needy.' When that happens, it is enough to recognise it for what this is—your ego-self talk—and you tell yourself, 'I care more about my client than what my ego tells me right now.' That way, you will learn to lead powerful sales conversations that will transform many lives.

For example, one of my gorgeous clients who I worked with for almost two years, emailed me frequently expressing the same fears.

- 'I am due to send the last reminder about my latest programme but I am so scared that many people will unsubscribe.'
- 'I plan to reach out to all the suitable candidates for my new course, but my mind is going crazy; do I really have to do this, and what will they think of me?'

Every time she emailed me she framed the same challenge. So I asked her, 'Darling, what do you care about most, the fear in your mind or your clients?' She learned to care more about the clients who needed her help, rather than her self-talk, discouraging her from selling and following up. She established a new motto; 'I am doing it for them! I love my clients more than my fears!' In spite of the fact that committed selling challenged and stretched her mind, she always overshot her goals. The result was that she grew her business from £5K a year to more than £500K a year, in the space of two years and she facilitated a huge amount of positive transformation among her clients.

Yes, magical things can happen when we start focusing more on our potential clients rather than how we come across. Think about the pain your ideal clients are experiencing right now. Focus on the growth, the change, the joy, the peace, the happiness your potential clients can experience as a result of investing in your service. Be more concerned about that than what your ego is shouting. Once you start selling regularly and often, your ego will go quiet. Selling will become a part of your comfort zone. Simply put, you will shun your ego with love for other people and action to help them.

Mantra to overcome this belief; *'I care more about my clients than my fears.'*

2. 'I am taking away from clients when they buy from me.'

This is one of those less obvious thought patterns that discourages us from selling and proudly offering our services to the world. It is easy to think this way. After all, when sales happen, you gain money. It doesn't mean however, that you are taking anything away from anyone. Your client gains too. Selling is a gain-gain experience, unless you frame it otherwise. It is important to be clear about what specifically your clients gain as a result of buying from you and what will be the return on their investment in your services: emotionally, spiritually, physically and financially. Plus, the moment your client invests in your high-end coaching or any other high-end service you provide, it can be truly transformative for them. Sure, they will be parting with money, but they are also investing in themselves. They are investing in their change and growth. It is the moment when they say to themselves, 'I believe I am worthy of this service and I will do what it takes to achieve the result I want.'

This often creates an immediate energy shift. It is not uncommon—in my experience—to sign up a new high-end client one day, only to hear from them that they made all the money back the next day. This is because when they commit to the sale their consciousness shifts too. It opens a new way of thinking, new ideas and new determination. In fact, the moment a client buys your high-end service is the moment when they are truly committing to their change, which is a critical element in every coaching or other transformative work. The moment of sale is when you exchange energy with your client for a common purpose. It is a give-give experience and the one that allows your clients to give themselves permission to succeed, which is absolutely priceless.

Mantra to overcome this belief; *'In the moment of sale, my clients grow their wings.'*

3. 'I'm scared that I won't be able to deliver.'

Your responsibility is to deliver world-class coaching or whatever service you provide. Unless you are contracted in a single service provider arrangement, it is assumed that your client will also need to do their part. For example, right now I am being coached by a top-notch book coach; is it her responsibility for this book to be written? No, not really; that responsibility rests with me. The responsibility of my professional book coach is to provide the guidance and feedback that will help me to write the book. In high-end coaching, the line between where the coach's responsibility ends and where the coachee's responsibility starts is not as obvious.

High-end coaching is about taking 100% responsibility for both parts, the coach and coachee. As coaches, we are 100% responsible to use our coaching skills to help clients gain clarity in their thinking; help them open up opportunities for the future; identify when they are limiting themselves; and help them find a way to become unstuck. It is our responsibility to be honest. I believe it is also our responsibility to continue working on developing our skills and improving ourselves as women and entrepreneurs, so we don't do disservice to our clients by hitting an energetic plateau. It is our client's responsibility, however to be: open to be challenged; voice problems; be honest; and implement agreed action steps.

Ultimately, it is our client's responsibility to create their results. When we take that responsibility off our high-end coaching clients, we become like overly protective mothers. We fall into fixing our clients and saving them, instead of empowering them to create the desired change in their businesses and lives. We take away from the client's tremendous power they have to alter any area of their lives. It is worthwhile to define your responsibilities, as well as your client's and communicate them clearly with your potential clients prior to their purchase.

Mantra to overcome this belief; *'I guide clients' transformations. My clients create those transformations.'*

4. 'I don't like following up on people. If they want to work with me, they will let me know.'

I spend a lot of time behind a computer desk and, as a result, I appreciate a good back massage. Admittedly, I only pick up the phone and book a treatment when I feel my back is in pain, when it hurts. Yep, self-care, as much as I know it, is important, but it is not my strongest trait. You know what is crazy? Until very recently, not once did I get a phone call or text from a massage therapist inviting me to return. Not once did a massage therapist take full control and made sure I received regular massages booked in as a schedule. I know I am writing from personal experience and—hopefully—not talking about all massage therapists, but let me tell you; I am grateful I have finally found a massage therapist who is great at following up. It saves me from regular back pain!

The same goes for coaching and other professional services. The vast majority of people will take action only when they are in their low, pain point, when they can't take a second longer experiencing their specific problem. It is our responsibility to help clients not to get to that point and follow up with them first. Following up is professional. It shows you care and most people will appreciate it. Your client can tell you at any time, 'No, thank you'. But mostly you will hear, 'Thank you for getting in touch again. I meant to call you, but...'

Mantra to overcome this belief; *'I follow up because I care.'*

5. 'My potential clients will be put off if I sell every day.'

Imagine visiting a shopping centre in your town, only to find the majority of shops closed with signs on the doors. 'We are closed today because we do not want to offend you with selling.' It would be ridiculous. Yet, it is exactly what is happening in the women's entrepreneurial space. We are often too shy to sell. Many women are shy to share with the world their paid programmes and services, unapologetically. I can say this because I used to be one of these women until that unfortunate £7.30 moment.

If that happens to be you, here is one loving suggestion. Remember that at any point, your potential clients have the choice to say, No. People can choose to unfollow you on social media, or unsubscribe from your mailing list, if they don't resonate with your message or with whatever you sell. People can say, 'No thank you' if you reach out to them and offer them solutions to their problems. And that No is completely okay. Your potential clients have a choice to say

No at any point of your sales process. Therefore, thinking you will put people off by selling every day is completely unsubstantiated.

We don't market and sell with the objective of convincing people to buy. In fact, whenever you have a feeling you are convincing people to buy from you, I suggest you back off. You are probably not right for each other, at least not in this very moment. For example, I remember being approached by a woman who was referred to me by one of my previous clients. When we talked on the phone, I noticed plenty of probing questions, such as, 'What is your typical client result? How many clients have you worked with?' After a while, I got a sense that this woman didn't trust me fully and I needed to convince her of the quality of my work. I decided to be completely honest with her. I suggested that she investigated the free materials on my website to get a sense of my work. I explained that under no circumstances can I guarantee results, except providing whatever guidance and coaching was necessary to create the results she wanted.

After only two days, this woman contacted me again with a request for another call. She became my client and we developed a thriving coaching relationship. However, it could have been a completely different story if I had only focused on trying to convince her to buy from me. That is not how we, extraordinary women entrepreneurs, behave. We professionally guide our potential clients to make the right choice for them, whether it is a Yes or a No. At the same time, a sales conversation is an opportunity for us to explore whether we are the right match for that particular client, whether we will enjoy working with them and be able to help them reach their highest potential.

We calibrate these critical points throughout each sales conversation, asking questions such as, 'Does it make sense?'; 'How does that sound to you?'; 'What are your thoughts?'; 'How does that feel?' Your potential clients are in charge of their decisions from the beginning of the sales process through to the end. They decide whether it is a Yes, or No, when it comes to purchasing your service. And by the way, it is a good idea to get used to hearing, No. The idea of rejection is one of the greatest fears of our ego-self, which can pinch you to start with. Yet, as long as you continue opening those doors, continue marketing and selling, you will find that for each, 'No, thank you', there are many more 'Yes please' responses from clients, who will not only love working with you, but will benefit big time.

Mantra to overcome this belief; *'I choose selling every day, because I choose love, success and growth every day.'*

EXTRAORDINARY GROWTH CHALLENGE:
SALES BELIEFS OVERHAUL

My darling, now that we have explored a range of the major limiting beliefs about selling, it is your turn to explore and adjust your sales belief system in detail. Give yourself a gift of time and write down a comprehensive list of your assumptions and beliefs about selling. Ask yourself, 'What do I believe about selling that prevents me from selling every day and achieving excellent results?' If you find you hold assumptions about selling that are not aligned with creating extraordinary growth in your business, follow these three simple steps to challenge and reframe these beliefs.

133

Step One
Ask yourself; 'Why might this not be true?'

For example, if you currently believe you are simply not good at selling, write down a list of reasons why this belief may not be valid, such as, 'I sell my ideas all the time and I am pretty good at it. Selling is a skill and I can learn any skill.' And so on.

Step Two
Ask yourself; 'How does my higher-self see this problem?'

Dissociating yourself from your programmed mind and seeing things from a higher perspective is an excellent way to reframe unhelpful ways of thinking. Write down whatever comes to your mind.

Step Three
Ask yourself; 'Why might the opposite be true?'

For example, if you previously believed that you are not good at selling, ask yourself: 'Why can I be good at selling?' Or, 'Why am I good at selling?' Make a comprehensive list of your answers. With each answer that you come up with, you are building an evidence list of your new belief. This—in turn—engages your Reticular Activating System, a part of your brain that among other things is always looking for closure. Even when you redirect attention elsewhere, your Reticular Activating System will continue searching for more evidence for your new belief, creating and reinforcing a new reality for you.

To make this work for you, I have a fabulous resource to help you reframe all limiting beliefs around selling very quickly. It is an audio recording containing Energetic Selling Mastery affirmations and a complete set of healthy sales beliefs. Visit energeticselling.com/resources and you will find this resource, among other book resources. Listen to this audio daily, and I know you will fall in love with selling in no time. Working on our beliefs about selling may seem intangible work, yet nothing could be further from the truth. Think about it; the power of belief helped mankind to land on the moon, to make ground-breaking discoveries and inventions, to develop miraculously cancer cures and other dangerous diseases.

When it comes to selling, sometimes shifting only one unhelpful belief can make all the difference. That is exactly what happened to one of my clients. She listened to one of my live training calls where I was talking about what selling is and what it is not. During that training call, she shifted her thinking from; 'Having sales conversations with people means I need to convince them of the quality of my work' to 'Having sales conversation with people is about exploration'. 'Oh, that's easy!' she told me afterwards and immediately invited a bunch of potential clients to have a chat with her. Within five days, seven of those clients had said, 'Yes please!' to her premium coaching programme. Yes, she got herself fully booked with high-end clients because of reframing a single sales belief in her mind! If your sales revenues are not exactly where you want them to be, it is time to explore your belief system, right now!

'The fastest way to fall in love with selling is by selling.'

Here is one caveat regarding working on your sales belief system. It won't work if you don't back it up by action. In fact, the fastest way to change your beliefs about selling is by selling daily. Commitment to selling is the key and this is the most important point when it comes to changing your relationship with it. No matter where your belief system is when it comes to selling right now, no matter how good, or not-so-good you are at selling, don't wait until you are fully aligned with the idea of selling before you do it daily. Sell daily, even if it is only for 10-20 minutes a day.

This can include:

- Reaching out to potential clients
- Giving direct calls to action in your marketing
- Following up with clients
- Pitching your services to relevant companies
- Getting on that phone and just doing it!

If you are not used to selling daily—as I wasn't—you may feel awkward or uncomfortable at first. This is purely because daily selling is not part of your conditioned-self. It is not part of your norm. Inevitably, selling will push you out of your comfort zone and make you feel different. Your ego-self may go a little crazy too. But that is okay because as long as you sell every day, with no exception for a prolonged period of time, you will not only improve your sales and communication skills profoundly, but you will fall in love with it. Taking action is the most powerful way to overcome any limiting belief. It is the most powerful way to harness the power of self-alignment. Start selling today and tomorrow and the day after. If you are not used to selling daily, this new habit—a habit of daily selling—will change everything for you and your business.

Active versus passive selling

'I am very committed to my business and doing what I can to grow, but I am stuck in one place.' I cannot tell you how many times I have heard this complaint from the most intelligent, gifted and hard-working women. Yet, when I start to question them about what specifically they do to attract their high-end clients, the list often goes something like this, 'I send out a newsletter once a week. I network a lot. I put social media posts on Facebook and Instagram, etc.' When you put out a social media post and then, cross your fingers and hope that someone will approach you; when you send out regular newsletters only to get disappointed at the lack of response; when you attend networking events only to never follow up on your new connections—you are only putting out the energy of passive selling. You are waiting and that is exactly what you will get more of—more waiting. Extraordinary growth is not based on waiting!

> *'Every marketing strategy needs to be backed*
> *up by active selling'*

Active selling—and extraordinary growth—is about:
• Giving individual people the opportunity to say Yes or No to you
• Opening metaphorical doors to your house, such as, 'Would you like to come in?'
• Reaching out to people you have a relationship with and you know you can help
• Following up with people who have expressed an interest in your work but never followed through
• Giving your current clients the opportunity to upsell to the next level of service

- Asking for recommendations
- Pitching your talks or services to larger organisations and strategic partners; and putting yourself out there, rather than waiting for people to approach you

When you take an active approach to selling, you are never waiting. Instead, you are creating. You decide what you want to create in your business; in the next two weeks; month; six weeks; eight weeks; or whatever time period is most appropriate for you. You create a plan and you lovingly sell every working day. This is the only way that growth in your business doesn't become only possible, but inevitable.

EXTRAORDINARY GROWTH CHALLENGE:
ACTIVE OUTREACH

So, my gorgeous, it is time to put your hand on your heart and ask yourself, 'Do I sell as often as needed to create the growth in my business I want?' If the answer to that question is No, perhaps it is time to commit to selling your genius daily. Your ego may hate it at first, but it will thank you later and your business with it. One of the best ways to start practicing your active selling muscle is with personal outreach. Review your contact list and the people you have met during the last twelve months or longer and decide who can you reach out to and: ask for a referral; follow up with; and offer your services?

Make a comprehensive list. Then, outreach to at least ten people during the next week and continue with this exercise until you exhaust your list. Then, do it all again and make a habit out of it. When you take this active action your business won't be able to stay where it is today. This is exactly what happened to Noha Essop, a business coach and NLP trainer, based in South Africa. After working in personal development and training facilitation for thirteen years, she decided it was time to spread her wings and grow her business big time. Having a sales background, she had the ability to sell ice to Eskimos—when selling for other people—but selling her own products was a completely different story. She avoided selling because of her fear of being pushy and she thought she had to outsource that aspect of her business.

By the way, outsourcing is fantastic and essential for healthy business growth too, but if you hate selling, guess how this is going to reflect back at you through the work of outsourced sales professionals? Probably not so well, which was Noha's experience and so, finally, she decided to make the necessary shifts in her mind for once and all. She joined the Extraordinary Growth Academy and immediately started to work on her relationship with selling. 'It finally clicked for me that selling is love made visible,' Noha recalled. She immediately started to practice active selling, and approached ten potential clients in the first week and six of those clients signed up for Noha's amazing training. Since then, she has refused to practice waiting in any capacity in her business, actively working on her energy behind selling, marketing and other aspects of the business. She increased her training fees by five times, expanded her clientele from local to global and, in her own words, 'I made a massive decision to choose courage not fear, growth not comfort, and my business keeps growing because of that.' Is it time for you to do the same, my darling?

IN THIS CHAPTER, YOU HAVE DISCOVERED

- Commitment to selling is a commitment to your higher-self and your extraordinary growth.
- What the major limiting beliefs are about selling and how to address them.
- The difference between active and passive selling.

Before we move onto the next chapter, ask yourself these three powerful questions.

1. What is my relationship with selling and how do I want to change it?
2. Where have I been practicing the energy of waiting in my business?
3. What activities fall under active selling in my business and how can I increase them?

In the next chapter, we will explore one unusual way to skyrocket your sales revenues. Let's do it!

8
DETACHMENT

THE UNUSUAL WAY TO SKYROCKET YOUR SALES REVENUES

*'It is only when you detach from specific outcomes
that your soul can express itself fully through you.'*

RUNNING THE FIRST Extraordinary Live Event—
a transformative weekend experience for 100 coaches and
change-makers was a huge stretch for me. I didn't want to
run a standard entrepreneurial event. I wanted to create the
most phenomenal experience for women that would
inevitably open the next level of consciousness and create
masses of opportunities for them for the year ahead.

As such, I decided to go for the very best—from the
venue through to a Master of Ceremonies, entertainment,
and anything else that comes with putting on an
unforgettable experience for entrepreneurs who are ready to
scale their impact. I was shaking when signing the venue
contract with the luxury hotel, but I did it; and I decided to
put my heart and soul into making it work. A few weeks later,
we opened the ticket sales. I was planning to sell the first 30
tickets in that first week, and I put a huge amount of energy
behind my marketing.

Naturally, it was very important to me and I had to make it work. But day one, no sales; day two, no sales; day three, no sales. By day seven, when the initial offer for the Extraordinary Live Event was expiring, two gorgeous women booked their tickets. Not exactly thirty, as I had planned, and my ego was going crazy, 'This is it. I am going to make a right fool out of myself when there will only be ten of us in the room. I may lose all my business because of it. Who the hell will want to learn from a failure of a woman like me? I have to make this work!' Yes, I was stressing big-style and taking things out of proportion. My husband, who was patiently listening, dropped a bomb at me, 'I hear you; and don't you think you are making it a little too much about yourself? Why not relax now? It's Saturday evening; you have done enough. Let those women who are supposed to be there, be there. How about having a glass of brandy with me, instead of working on it now?'

And I did exactly that, because my husband was right. I was so wrapped up in my fear of failure and the urgency to make it work that I was caught up in 'it's all about me' thinking. I changed it there and then. I assumed that whatever will or won't happen, will be for the benefit of all. Those women who are called to be at the Extraordinary Live Event and will benefit tremendously, will be there. And I sure as hell am not going to help it while putting out there, 'I need to pay a hefty hotel bill' energy. In other words, I detached from the outcome and 'surrendered upwards.'

About thirty minutes later, a notification popped up on my smart phone. Vivienne Joy, a business coach for women, expressed how the Extraordinary Live Event was calling her, but there was no way she could justify the investment. I am not sure if I felt empowered by the resolution I had made after my husband gave me his piece of mind, or a glass of brandy, or both, but I challenged her thinking, 'Vivienne, are you and your business not worth an extra few hundred pounds?' She decided to talk to her partner, who reminded her, 'Of course, you are worth it!' Later that evening, she booked her VIP ticket. Not only that, she booked a luxury room in the hotel. She attended the Extraordinary Live Event, and the changes she made as a result of that weekend were, in her own words, 'Breath-taking'. She immediately increased her fees five times and created heartfelt programmes that attracted clients who were ready to be served at that level. This alone took her business to a brand new, exciting level.

Now here is the thing. Had I been still wrapped up in, 'I need to make this work' thinking, I would probably have started seriously considering dropping the investment fees for the Extraordinary Live Event, which would not only have hurt my business, but ultimately, all the women who wanted to attend. Instead, I got completely detached from the outcome and challenged Vivienne on her limiting ways of thinking, which were keeping her small. With this energetic shift, we sold out the rest of the tickets in a good time and had the most transformative experience on the planet. So much so, that I decided to make Extraordinary Live an annual event.

This is a small example of how attaching to certain sales outcomes affects our personal energy and consequently, profoundly influences the quality of our sales conversations, and the results we achieve through our selling activities. Following on from the previous chapter, where we tackled a selection of the major limiting assumptions about selling, this chapter will explore one of the concepts that is not commonly talked about in sales training; detachment. You will discover how practicing this principle in fullness will enable you to show up at your best when talking to prospective clients, address common sales objections such as, 'I can't afford you' or 'I will have to think about it' confidently and send your sales revenues through the roof.

> *'Detachment is not that you should own*
> *nothing. But that nothing should own you.'*
> *Ali ibn abi Talib*

There isn't one spiritual scripture that doesn't talk about the importance of detachment. Even the Buddha proclaimed: *'upadhi dukkhassa mūlanti'*, which in English means 'Attachment is the root of all suffering.' If you think about this long enough, you will probably acknowledge that this is true for you too. It is only when we expect certain outcomes and not get exactly what we expect, or in a way we expect, that we start engaging in worrying, internal battling, judging ourselves or other people and buy into the myth of failure.

Unfortunately, practically all of us have been programmed to practice attachment. We were expected to excel in school exams because the opposite may be met with harsh words from parents; and we become attached to the way we look because we want to be liked. We get attached to the achievement of our future ambitions because fulfilment of them will bring us a sense of accomplishment and not achieving them would mean that forbidden word; failure. And then, we have responsibilities. We have bills to pay, families to look after, a lifestyle to maintain. No wonder it's so easy to catch ourselves thinking, 'I hope this conversation with a prospective client will end up in a sale.'

And yet, it is exactly this type of thinking—insisting on a certain outcome—that can hinder the quality of your sales conversation and your sales revenues big time. When you are attached to a specific sales outcome, your prospective clients will—consciously or unconsciously—pick up on it. The conversation will have an undertone of 'this is more about me rather than about you' and that energy is not exactly inviting for your potential clients. Furthermore, attachment can hinder your listening ability, creative thinking and coming up with solutions for your clients. As a result, it is possible that sales conversations can leave you feeling depleted, or even having a sense of failing.

Completely detaching from outcomes while selling, on the other hand, will leave your prospective client feeling, 'This person is trying to help me.' You will be much more present during those sales conversations, much more honest, much better equipped to address your client's objectives—unexpressed fears—with love. Perhaps paradoxically, you will enjoy a lot more 'Yes please, let's do it' responses to your offers than before.

How do we detach, then? How do you make sure you practice the art of detachment while talking to your prospective clients? The answer to this question lies in one word: presence. Presence is the antidote to attachment. When you are fully present, you are not thinking about your responsibilities, how you need to perform, past, or future. You are fully focused on your prospective client. They become the centre of your universe for a while. You listen and observe your prospective client more attentively, your creative thinking improves and your intuition gets sharper. You will know exactly what to say and how to say it to empower your client and you will find solutions for their problems. Sales professionals who are fully present 'become the value themselves, work with buyers collaboratively, and create real change for their customers.'[5] In other words,

[5] Schultz, Mike and Doerr, John E. (2014). Insight Selling: Surprising Research on What Sales Winners Do Differently. Hoboken, New Jersey: John Wiley & Sons

your clients will be able to tune into your real energy, and that becomes your currency. This is not possible when you are focused on your ego-thoughts. Moreover, when you are fully present, your client will feel heard and understood. This alone will create a real connection between you and your client, and has the potential to increase your sales conversions big style.

I helped Joel improve her selling skills. She was a dedicated learner, and studied a number of selling courses and read a ton of books on a topic of sales. But her sales conversion was very poor. She had to go through a ton of sales conversations to land a single client. I encouraged her to role model her typical sales conversation with me. Two minutes into this basic exercise, I understood why she had trouble selling. Her dedication to master selling skills led her to write a sales script, including the exact questions to ask, the exact things to say, in a specific order. She read the questions of her script and as I answered, she promptly moved onto a next question. I said: 'Stop now, I might as well talk to a robot.' Those were perhaps harsh words, but that was exactly the feeling I was having. During the next few months, we worked on moving this thinking from her head to her heart. She ditched the scripts, and practiced the art of presence. Naturally, the more present she became, the bigger sales conversions she enjoyed.

'All you seek is here, now.'

Never wait until the next sales conversation to practice the art of presence. Take time before each sales conversation and remind yourself of the following powerful principles that will centre you, empower you, and focus your attention on here and now.

146

1. Your sales goals are merely quantum symbols

I am a huge fan of setting powerful sales intentions. Personally, I go as far as dividing our company sales goals into weeks and days. This helps me to stay focused and make my selling activity one of my daily priorities. In Chapter Nine, I will guide you to set powerful, unique financial intentions that will be aligned with your extraordinary growth, and as a result, increase the chances of achieving your goals with ease.

While setting short-term sales goals is a powerful way to keep your mind focused, it has a potential downside. It invites your human mind to attach to the outcome. It is important, therefore, that you learn to completely detach from your short-term goals. You see, we set our goals using our conscious mind. We set them based on what we think we need, want, and are capable of achieving. We often take into account our past performance, trends, and the current climate in the market. Your higher-self, however, has its own agenda. And it is much more expansive, much more exhilarating than what your programmed mind can currently perceive.

In fact—and most people don't realise this—your programmed physical mind is incapable of generating ideas; your higher mind does that. Your brain receives vibration of that idea and your physical mind perceives it. That is how ideas are born and brought to reality. Your higher-self conceives them, your brain receives them and your programmed-self perceives them. As a result, much can be lost in translation. Your higher mind may plan a feast, but you would prefer a picnic in the park. And if that picnic in the park doesn't happen exactly as you planned, you may be disappointed. But your higher-self rejoices because she knows

147

that as you leave that picnic, you will get exactly to the place where the feast happens.

This is why I like to call our goals *quantum symbols*. They merely represent which direction our higher-self is calling us. For example, you might set a goal to launch and sell out a specific programme. You know exactly how many clients you want to serve this way, at what fees you want to sell this programme, and how much profit you will want to make. But how the hell do you know whether this is exactly the right goal for you? Why not one client more, or one dollar more? How do you know it is not meant to be one client less, or one dollar less? How would you know if this specific goal is exactly in the alignment with your extraordinary growth? The truth is, you don't, not consciously. Perhaps, you are meant to serve twice more clients through that programme. Or perhaps half the clients you plan, so you can have space to receive an idea, and implement the idea that will take your business much further than running the programme in its full capacity. The chances are that you will achieve some of your sales goals exactly as you planned; you will overachieve others; and you won't achieve some too. And that is okay, as long as you surrender upwards, do your part fully, take everything as a gift, learn from each experience, and allow yourself to grow more for it.

This is exactly what happened to Sarah. She felt called to create a group online programme for her clients. She put a lot of energy into creating the programme, writing amazing sales pages, marketing the programme and outreaching to prospective clients who would benefit hugely. Every day, she would connect with the energy of achieving her goal and let her intuition guide her. And yet at the end she sold only very few places, less than 10% of what she planned.

Sarah could easily have become discouraged and consider this a failure but far from it. You see, as she was taking inspired action to achieve this goal, something else happened. She became fully booked with her high-end clients, meaning that she created much more revenue than she planned; and she worked with her clients on a much deeper level, which was her zone of genius. In addition, she received feedback from prospective clients that rather than large group programmes, they would benefit from intimate group programmes, with more 1-2-1 attention. Later on, Sarah did exactly that. She created, launched and sold out a high-end Mastermind programme, which attracted perfect clients for her, reduced her 1-2-1 coaching time dramatically and increased her revenues by as much. Sarah expanded her capacity to serve and created extraordinary growth in her business but in a very different way than she previously planned.

Therefore, whenever you set a short-term goal, it is important to tell yourself, 'I will get that, or much better'. You do your bit. Connect with the higher aspect of yourself every day; listen out for inspired action and implement. Market, sell, learn, and be dedicated to achieving your intention. At the same time, let the universe do its bit. Let it stir you in the exact direction that will enable you to expand in ways you could never even imagine. As well as you let go of what, let go of how. You see, your higher mind is not somebody else. It is you. That is why we call this aspect of your being your higher-self. In fact, your higher-self is much wiser than your programmed-self.

Your higher-self has a real point of view, she knows—or more precisely you know on that level—what is your big goal, and exactly how to get there step by step. It communicates that goal to your physical-self and each step of how to get there. But you cannot hear the whole sentences, the whole plan. All you will receive is the representation of your big goal, and urges, nudges to move in this or that direction. And that is okay.

Lastly, you will want to detach from timing. If you are in a room with 50 CEOs of multi-million companies and ask them this question: 'How many times did you grow your sales revenues by exactly as much as you planned, in exactly the time frame you planned?', you know what 50 of those CEOs would answer? Zero. No matter how thoughtful your plan might be, it is coming from the physical mind's perspective; the somewhat limited perspective.

By the way, I am a huge fan of plans and strategies, because they are fantastic ways to give us a sense of clarity. They align our physical mind with compelling goals. But when that plan doesn't work out exactly as we planned? If our timing is off track it's okay! The universe is never late— you will get what you choose exactly when is perfect for you—not one second before, not one second after. So, bask in the excitement of what is coming and stay flexible when parts of your strategies don't work out exactly as planned.

One way to practice detachment from sales goals is to swap short-term financial goals for creating a huge goal—as big as you can perceive right now—and focus on it every day, with an intention to achieve this goal as fast as possible. In this case, your unique mantra that you want to keep on the top of your mind will sound something like this. 'I am creating ten million pounds worth of impact in the world right now, and it is unfolding in a way that is for the highest good of myself and others.'

Contemplate on that mantra often. Create a picture of a ten million pound company in your mind and work backwards. Make sure you embody the energy of that goal

150

every day and track your progress towards it. That way, your higher-self will provide your with ideas to help you to make it happen, connect you with people who will help you to make it happen, and uncover the opportunities for your growth. Whether you set for yourself a short-term or long-term sales intentions, or both, remember that they are quantum symbols and exactly that, or that far better is planned for you. Allow yourself to receive it.

2. You cannot lose the right client

Take the pressure off yourself, and the need to get it right with your sales conversations. The truth is, you do not need any specific client to create extraordinary growth in your business. Even if you have only one sales conversation scheduled, reframe from thinking, 'I need this sale so I hope this call will go well'. Direct your awareness to the knowing that there are, in any given moment, more perfect-for-you clients that you can serve right now, as they are a reflection of your consciousness. This is truth even if you are not aware of those clients consciously.

Go to each sales conversation as an explorative experience and the one that will help your prospective clients to highlight their choices. It is up to them how they decide. It is not your responsibility to decide in the right way. And even if you assume after the sales call is completed that you could have done much better in terms of holding energy for your client, be assured that you simply cannot lose the right client. Perhaps you are not exactly the right match for each other right now. Perhaps there is something else for you to learn or experience to be able to serve them powerfully. The chances are, a lot of those No responses will turn to Yes responses later on anyway.

151

It happened to me early on in my online business; I went through nineteen sales conversations within two weeks, only to book exactly zero clients. The truth is, my energy was all over the place at that time. I wasn't present enough for my prospective clients. I was thinking more about, 'I need to make this work.' Regardless of the many selling mistakes I made during that two week period, over 50% of those clients hired me as their coach within the next six months. And of course, once you take the pressure of yourself to perform well, or to the need to get it right, you increase your presence during sales conversations and your clients will feel it. Completely detaching from the outcome and from your need to perform will allow you to say to your clients such powerful things as:

- 'Whether you decide this is the right opportunity for you today or not, it is perfect.'
- 'I am not sure I can help you at this point.'
- 'From what you are saying, I don't get a sense you need help; am I missing something?'
- 'I don't feel we are right for each other at this point; here is what I suggest instead.'

Say those things when appropriate. Contrary to what we might think, this builds tremendous trust with your clients. They will appreciate your honesty, be more open with you and even when they don't become your high-end client, they will gladly recommend other people to you.

For example, I once had a sales conversation with a well-known divorce lawyer and the founder of *Project of Positive Change*, Leigh Daniels. She was nearing US$400K in revenues per year, and she enquired about working with me following a talk I had given. From speaking with her, it was not immediately obvious to me how I could help her; and that was exactly what I told her: 'I am not convinced you need my help.' Leigh said, 'Really? But I truly feel I could benefit from working with you.' She then opened up about her struggles and how she wanted to grow her company, but was at her full capacity and felt exhausted. This additional information—that she wasn't previously ready to share—gave me a deeper insight into the workings of her mind and I immediately understood how I could help her solve her problems. We ended up working together for a year, restructuring the way she worked and functioned internally, and in that time Leigh crossed to seven-figure annual revenue with ease.

3. Sales conversations are a welcomed pattern-interrupter for your potential clients

Sometimes you end up having a sales conversation with a client because they have been recommended to you. Other times because you reached out to them specifically, or made a public offer with a call to action to reach out to you. It doesn't matter how you end up talking with your prospective clients; in each case, the fact is that they are talking to you because they are currently running an undesirable pattern they wish to break. Perhaps they have been procrastinating from writing that book forever; or experienced a stream of unhealthy relationships; or their body is not in the best shape and it is troubling them. They are running an unhealthy pattern and they need to change. They need help.

As a result, you can go into the sales conversation assuming that you will indeed be working together, unless it transpires that you are not a perfect match right now. In other words, talk to your prospective clients as if you were their coach already. This will help you to refrain from pleasing your clients or proving how amazing a coach you are, instead, focusing on how you can make an impact in their lives by highlighting their unhealthy patterns, and bringing to the forefront what exactly what they need to do to permanently change. Bringing proving energy into sales conversations is very unhealthy—both for yourself and your prospective client. When you think, 'I will give them a taste of what an amazing coach I am' you will be tempted to fix their life within an hour, or however long you are working together—which, of course, is impossible—and can easily create the so called Fast Food Effect. Your prospective client will think they now have all they need to succeed, go off, start implementing, and oftentimes stop at the first hurdle, assuming 'it didn't work for me.'

While sales conversation interrupts your prospective clients' unhealthy patterns, it is your service, whether it is coaching or something else, that creates and reinforces a new pattern. Be honest about this when talking to your clients, 'As your coach, these are the areas we would need to address for you to get what you want.' Call them out on where they are holding onto unhealthy ways of thinking, exactly as you would during any other coaching session.

For example, shifting from proving to impacting made Allison Sarah McGinlay fully booked with her dream clients. She is a relationship coach who has been helping women save their marriage when considering divorce. Her work is incredibly powerful, but she realised that when she was talking to prospective clients, she would aim to please them, rather than empower them. What needed to be said was never said, and lots of clients ended their conversation with, 'I'll have to think about it' only to get back to her later and decline, saying now was not a good time.

154

Once Allison learned about the principle 'Don't aim to prove, aim to create an impact', she applied it right away. When her prospective clients gave her reasons for why they wanted to divorce and Allison knew these were unhealthy reasons, she could tell them exactly as it was and how they would most likely carry these issues into their post-divorce life and future relationships. This dose of healthy truth meant that clients realised what they were doing to themselves and how important it was to change the way they approached their relationships. Allison's sales conversion rates went through the roof, and before long she was fully booked with high-end clients. Needless to say, thanks to Allison's work there are many marriages thriving that would otherwise have ended.

I encourage you, my dear reader, to reflect on where could you be a little more honest with your prospective clients. Instead of getting guided by your ego thinking, 'Oh, I can't possibly say that, I will put them off.' By being their coach and aiming to create an impact, not only will your sales conversion improve, but many lives with it too.

4. Presence builds trust

When you are fully focused on your client, it encourages them to fully open up and share with you the deepest workings of their mind. Attentive listening, eye contact and 'Thank you for sharing that with me', can go a long way in achieving that. For many people, talking to you will be the first time when someone keenly listened to them and created space for them to be clear about what they truly want, what is bothering them, and what they need to change to solve their problem.

However, never simply ask, 'What do you want as a result of working together?' With that, they will probably only give you surface reasons, such as, 'I'd like more clients, a healthy relationship, etc. etc.', Ask them about *why* they want it, to understand their deeper desires. Never ask about their challenges and where they need help; help them realise exactly how these problems impact their lives, physically, emotionally, spiritually and financially. Yes, there is also a cost of *not* working with you and it can be very empowering for the client to realise what that cost is. Technically speaking, the sale happens when the value of your offering exceeds the real or perceived cost in the mind of your client. When they are sure you can help them to solve their burning problem. The trouble is, there are probably hundreds of other providers who can do that. Ultimately, your client will decide whether to work with you or not with their feelings.

For example, a fellow coach sent me a message saying, 'I received quotes from two copywriters to write three funnels for me. One quoted me £3.5K, the other £20K. Even though a lot more costly, I am much more drawn to the £20K copywriter, because I feel a sense they truly understand me.' Do not underestimate the power of creating a genuine emotional connection through your presence. It is truly one of the most powerful sales—and coaching—tools on the planet.

5. Sales conversations are a two-way exploratory experience

The purpose of the sales conversation is not only for your client to determine whether you are the right coach for them right now. It goes the other way too. As such, keenly listen to your intuition when you are talking to your prospective client, so you can be sure that you can not only contribute to your client tremendously, but also that you will enjoy working with them and they have characteristics of highly coachable clients. Ask them questions such as:

- 'If we were to work together, what would you be wiling to do, and not willing to do, to achieve your goal?'
- 'What threats do you see ahead, if we were to work together?'
- ' What makes you a great client?'

This type of question will metaphorically turn the tables around and gives your prospective client an opportunity to sell themselves.

6. Make an offer only when your client is ready to buy

'I have this service, would you like to buy it?' is probably not the place you will want to find yourself when facilitating a sales consultation. Having to convince someone that your product is right for them is the surest way to kill a client's trust in you and your confidence with it. And yet, that is exactly where we often put ourselves when we are attached to a certain sales outcome. Instead, make an offer to your client only after you are sure they are the perfect client for you and are ready to completely surrender to the process. Ask questions such as:

- 'Why do you want to work on these things now? Why not six months ago? Why not six months into the future?'
- 'Are you willing to invest time and money into making x happen during the next y months?'
- 'How committed are you to turn your situation around from 0-10? If not 10, why? How can you demonstrate your commitment?'

Only when you are sure your prospective client demonstrates that they are ready to work on changing their situation, describe your programme and how it can help them to bridge from where they are, to where they want to be.

7. Sales objections are fears, unexpressed

You are probably not an entrepreneur if you haven't met with this scenario at least once. You are having an amazing sales conversation with your prospective client. Everything is going great and you are sure you are talking to a perfect-for-you client. Then, when it comes to their decision, the bomb drops: 'I would love to work with you, but I cannot afford you.' Your heart sinks for a moment, and you quickly run through in your mind 70,390,000 search results when you Googled: 'How to overcome pricing objections?'

The thing is, it is nearly impossible to address your clients' sales objections with words alone, and it is absolutely impossible to successfully address them by relying on sales techniques alone. A change of attitude is needed in the first place. We can feel disappointed when we hear client's sales objections only if we are considering them to be something they are not, an obstacle for sale, or even, 'a polite way to say No'. But what if their sales objections were, in fact, expressing their interest in what you are offering and actually they are asking for help? You see, just like both your programmed-self and your higher-self are involved in the selling process, so it is the same for your client. They are listening and speaking as the whole person. Their higher mind may excitedly scream Yes, but when it comes to the moment of decision, their ego-self will panic: 'Change on the horizon! Danger!' And it will offer whatever is available to stop the client from committing to change, for example sales objections, such as, 'I can't afford it'. 'I will have to think about it.' 'I will have to talk to my partner.' 'I don't have time for it.'

However, given that you have practiced presence throughout your sales conversation and offered your prospective client your service only after you were sure there is a perfect match, the sales objections will be, in the vast majority of cases, merely unexpressed fears. And you want to treat your client's sales objections as such. You want to acknowledge that while they are expressing a surface problem, there is a deeper fear that needs to be addressed.

So, the first thing you want to do with any sales objection is to acknowledge and isolate them. 'Thank you for sharing that with me. May I ask, is this the only issue here?' Secondly, once they confirm, you want to bring your client's attention to the fact that most objections are actually covered fears. For example, 'In my experience, when someone says at this point that they can't afford it, in the vast majority of the cases it is not as much about the inability to finance the project, but rather about an unaddressed fear. Does this resonate with you?' Finally, let your clients empty their deeper feelings and then, help them overcome the real fear. Eight out of ten times, you will find the real fear your prospective clients have is that they are not trusting themselves—or you—enough to achieve the desired outcome.

This process is incredibly simple. But why is it that so many powerful women have trouble addressing these client sales objections? The first reason is that we often consider sales objections as something set in stone, as truth. Secondly, we are often influenced by our own ego. And that is the main thing you want to detach from when hosting powerful sales conversations: your own ego. Your intuition will guide you through the call, but so will your ego. Who will you listen to?

Buying into our ego and not asking that uncomfortable question, not challenging your perfect-for-you clients on their erroneous assumptions, not being completely honest with them can be costly because if you are not willing to go there, someone else will.

I recall a client called Rebecca who once said, 'I'd love to do this but I don't think I can afford you.' I took this powerful woman through the simple process above, making sure that her only issue was money, brought her attention to the fact that the unaffordability was probably masking an unresolved fear and coached her through it. In the end she said, 'Thank you. Thank you for calling me out on my fears. Another coach I talked to before you told me that I am simply not ready, and that was that.' She then became my client; and while she invested in coaching heavily, it proved to be a very profitable investment for her.

Remember, my darling: when you detach from your ego, from your need to get it right and from the specific outcome, you will tap into sales abilities you never knew you had. Yes, you are naturally very good at selling and practicing the art of presence will bring this skill of yours into the forefront.

Here is another good example, from Karen Baines who surrendered upwards and as a result her sales conversion and marketing results skyrocketed. Karen is a conscious karmic creation coach for women entrepreneurs. She shared with me during our initial sales conversation, 'My previous coach told me that the online world is not my natural habitat. Perhaps she is right, because I don't know anything about online marketing. But I have a deep calling to serve influencers globally and I would love to increase my income and be able to retire my husband.'

In fact, Karen simply needed to go through the discomfort of the learning curve and open herself up to serving a global audience. She did so and she became very successful. So much so that she was able to retire her husband, as her deep desire, within six months. However, soon after that she made a few costly decisions that set her a few steps back, and her business hit a growth plateau. As a result, we started actively working—both from an energetic and a strategic point of view—to create the next quantum leap in her business. Within the next few months, Karen expanded her team, built automated funnels, created and implemented a new online visibility strategy, actively outreached to prospect clients every day, as well as working on her personal energy through many tools outlined in this book.

However, nothing seemed to be shifting, and a number of times Karen came to her coaching sessions frustrated because her sales were not growing even though she followed all the advice. I had to remind Karen several times: 'Stay on course, and trust.' and on course she stayed. Incredibly, from one day to another, her business started to shift dramatically. Her online funnels started to convert like crazy—82% landing page conversion rate, which in marketing world is more than outstanding—clients started to reach out to her with a request for discovery calls at a rate she could not handle, and practically all the potential clients she had been talking to said Yes to one of her high-end offerings right away.

She told me, 'It feels like all the cosmic tumblers have clicked into place and the avalanche of gorgeous clients and abundance has been released. This level of growth is well beyond my expectation and one of the major shifts that helped me was that I learned to enjoy every second of the sales conversations with potential clients, without being fixed on the outcome. This has had a huge impact on the quality of my sales conversations, sales conversion, my confidence as a coach and on the growth of my business.' Karen knows that each sales conversation will end up with either Yes, No, or a gift—an important learning given to yourself by your higher-self, moving you along the path of extraordinary growth in ways that you can often not even imagine. When you choose presence not attachment, the very same will transpire for you, my darling.

EXTRAORDINARY GROWTH CHALLENGE:
MINDFUL PRESENCE

Practise this exercise before you start a sales conversation with your potential client. It will help you to detach from your ego, the outcome and be fully present for the client, so you can serve them in the most powerful way:

First, close your eyes and focus for two minutes on your breathing. Your mind may be wondering from time to time and that is okay. When you notice it, bring your attention back to your breathing. This is the basic form of practicing the mindful presence and the more you practice this, the easier it gets.

Second, set an intention such as, 'I will serve this client on the highest level possible. I care more about this client than I care about my fears, desires and needs. I will guide this client to make the right decision for them. I cannot lose the right client.'

Third, imagine green energy expanding from your heart towards the heart of your potential client. Create heart-to-heart connection.

This three minute exercise will help you to stay present during your sales conversations, become aware when your ego interferes with the process and serve the client in the most powerful way. The more you practice this, the more powerful your sales conversations will become and there is only one way your sales revenues can go with practicing the art of presence: up, up, and up.

IN THIS CHAPTER, YOU HAVE DISCOVERED

- Your goals are merely a representation of where your higher-self is calling you to go.
- You cannot lose the right client.
- Detachment is the unusual and very effective way to increase your sales revenues rapidly.
- Aiming to make an impact is far more powerful than aiming to prove your competence.
- Presence builds trust and helps you to detach from ego-thoughts.
- Sales objections are unexpressed fears.

Before you move onto the next part of the book, ask yourself these three questions.

1. Where in my business am I getting attached to: a specific outcome; the how; the timing; my performance; my ego-thoughts? Make a list of them.
2. With each answer on your list, ask yourself: 'Why, what is the reason for attaching to this?'
3. The question above will reveal your limiting ways of thinking. Follow up on each reason by exploring: 'How can I change this?' You might find it useful to apply a process of overhauling limiting beliefs to these reasons, as described in the previous chapter.

163

My dear reader, you are now ready to upgrade your money consciousness and leap into extraordinary growth. That is exactly what we are going to do in the final part of this book!

PART THREE

LEAP INTO
EXTRAORDINARY GROWTH

9
UPGRADE YOUR MONEY
CONSCIOUSNESS
AND BECOME A MONEY MAGNET

*'You are either money's bitch, or you
make money your bitch.'*

MY DEAR READER, I have a question for you. If you decided to triple your average monthly income in the next 30 days and keep it that way, what do you think needs to happen? Do you need to triple the amount of your marketing and sales activity; or triple the amount of other actions you take? Do you need to find a missing link that you are not aware of? Do you need to triple your advertising budget? Or do you need to do something else?

This is the exact question I asked my coach at the beginning of July 2015. I was entering the third month of my online coaching business. I was absolutely determined to create my first £20K month, which was more than three times the revenue I had ever taken in a one month and it was a lot of money in my mind at that point. 'You don't need to triple your doing. Instead, go back to basics and address your relationship with money. Pay more attention to your energy, and triple your financial thermostat.' This was as her answer.

I took that advice to heart. I didn't do anything differently from what I had done in any other month prior to that, but I spent more time on changing and upgrading how I applied my personal energy around the topic of money. It worked. That month, I made more than £20K with ease. In fact, I couldn't quite believe how easy it was. It felt like the most ideal clients and money found me, instead of me having to work hard for them. Through that experience I was totally sold on the importance of money consciousness and how it affects our business growth. Since then, I have tripled my business a few times. Of course, along the way I had to make various strategic decisions and changes in my business. But I can say with full integrity that paying attention and continually upgrading my consciousness around money has played a big part in my business growth.

You see, every time we have a calling to serve at a higher place and to take our business to the next level, it requires us to shift our relationship with money to the next level too. Without doing so would be like trying to fit the elephant—limitless abundance that is available to us at all times—through a tiny keyhole. We need a great big hole and we want to be channels of abundance, wide and open to receive. In the following pages, you will discover exactly how to do that. You will be introduced to a four step process and seventeen practices, to help you open yourself to receive abundantly and multiply your ability to earn by doing what you love. However, please note that this is not financial advice. Instead, the simple processes that I am about to share with you tackle money from an energetic perspective and have helped many people dramatically improve their financial reality. If this is something you are interested in, you will find these processes the most useful. They will expand your thinking; guide you to practice the energy of abundance and growth; and inspire you to take aligned action.

Right now, I invite you to do what my coach advised me to do several years ago. Go back to basics, address your relationship with money, and increase your financial thermostat. It doesn't matter how much money you already make, or how much money you want to make, these processes are simple, fun and universal. They can unlock the doors to a brand new financial reality for you.

Step One: Take control of your money

Exactly like anything else, the basis of money is energy. Money is neutral energy and does not care how smart you are; smart and not-so-smart people can make lots of money. It doesn't care how diligent you are; hard working and lazy people can make lots of money. Money doesn't care whether your chakras are aligned, or whether you have earned your right to make lots of money through years of hard work. It doesn't care about any of that. What it does care about is how you relate to it: how you think about money, feel about money, speak about money and how you treat money. Money only cares about how you apply your energy around the topic of money and it mirrors back at you your relationship with it. The amount of money that flows through you is an exact reflection of your money consciousness. Now, when you decide to change your money consciousness, or take it to the next level, a great starting point is to acknowledge how you are relating to money right now.

Sometimes I ask my clients the following question: consider your relationship with money. If you were to personify it, what kind of relationship would it be? What role would money play in your life?

Many people say, 'Money is a rare visitor I never see around.' Other people consider money like a drug dealer: 'I'm addicted to money—shortly after I get a fix, I crave the next one.' There are people who view money as: good friends; lovers; teachers; and unattainable love interests. You name it and yes, it is a good idea to name your relationship with money, so you know where you are at right now.

Either way, there are only two ways to relate to money. You either control money, or it controls you. If you are in full control of money, you know exactly how money behaves in your life. You are aware how much money is coming in and how much money is going out. You check your accounts, statements and investments etc. regularly. You open your bills when they arrive, and you pay them on time. You don't make decisions based on money itself. But you make decisions and then, instruct money to adjust, with your full co-operation, of course. When you are in full control of money, you feel good about money because, after all, money does not affect how you feel about it. You like money and are always happy to make and to receive more of it.

When money controls you instead of you controlling the money, it can be a completely different story. Even the thought of money can make you uncomfortable. Yes, money can control how you feel. You avoid it. Unopened envelopes with the bills piling up. You don't like checking your bank balance, or spending, or knowing how much money you owe and how you are going to repay it. Why should you? It makes you feel uncomfortable! So, you had better continue avoiding it. And you are often pissed off about money because there is never enough of it, or just enough, but never quite as much as you would like. Which category are you? Are you controlled by money or does it control you; or a little of both?

The first step to creating the money shift and becoming a powerful money magnet is to be in absolute control of it. You don't want to be a bitch to money. You want to make money your bitch. If you recognise that money controls you to any extent, then it is time to change that relationship and become a master of your money. Here is how you can do that.

1. Know your money situation
Feelings aside, it is time to look at your money head on. Print the bank statements from the last three months. Calculate how much money exactly came into your account every month, and what are your money sources. Tackle your expenses. How much money do you spend on average each month and on what, specifically? Calculate your breakeven point, the amount of money you need to make each month to meet your current needs and lifestyle.

2. Eliminate the money leaks
As you go through your monthly expenditure, pay attention to subscriptions, memberships and other direct debit items you no longer use. Also, notice if there are any deducted payments that should not be there. I recall one woman, Jody, who (reluctantly) started to tackle her money like this, and when she went through her bank statements, she noticed a £7,000 charge that was fraudulent. Can you believe that? But the good news is that of course she managed to get that money back. Another client eliminated more than £500 of unused membership fees; quite a big money leak, gone!

3. Tackle your debt
Now it is time to look at your debt, if you have any, and tackle it head-on. Look at how much money you owe and

create a plan for paying it off consistently. One of the best ways is to set a specific percentage of your income that you automatically pay off with each incoming payment. Some years ago, I accumulated thousands of pounds of debt on credit cards. I paid the minimum amount each month by direct debit, but nothing more, because I felt I didn't have the money to spare. Eventually, I cut up the credit card so I could not use it, but the debt dragged along with me for several years.

Then I read the book *The Richest Man in the Babylon*, which I highly suggest you read. In spite of my financial difficulties, I followed the advice I discovered, and I paid 30% of my income towards my credit card debt each month. Strangely, not only did I survive and paid off my credit cards much faster than I predicted, but something else happened. My income started to grow too. Looking back, I know why. You see, when you spend money responsibly, which paying off your debts certainly is, you automatically create a vacuum and our nature is to fill vacuums. Plus, money loves responsibility. By stretching myself and paying off my credit cards debts, I also started to increase the flow of money; a concept I will explain later in this chapter.

Whatever percentage you set as an automatic payment towards your debts, make sure you stretch yourself, and in time the money will thank you for it. Also, while we are on the subject of debt: it is important to shed your guilt around having one. Debt is not a dirty word. For many new entrepreneurs or those entrepreneurs who want to scale up their business, funding is the only way, or certainly a much faster way, to make it happen. I too, used debt to fund the growth of my business on several occasions and I am glad I did. It was a calculated risk that I was willing to take. The word responsibility is the key here. Always, forgive yourself for how you accumulated your debt; set a plan for paying it off, and resolve to use debt responsibly in future.

Step Two: Set powerful money intentions

Money loves a home. It loves having a purpose. In other words, it is not enough to want to make more money for the purpose of having more money. There is no 'juice' in that. Instead, set a powerful money intention. That way, you will increase your chances of shifting your money reality manifold. Here is a guide of how to do that.

1. Practice no-limits thinking
Close your eyes for a moment and imagine what your life would be like if money was flowing through you in limitless amounts. Now, with that in mind, where are you living? How are you going about your business? How are you showing up in the world and serving other people? What are you wearing? How are you spending your time? While money cannot change our character, it can certainly allow us to live in our fullness. It is important to realise and regularly tune into what your potential really is. That way, you practice the energy of abundance and let the universe reflect it back to you through your business and through the status of your bank account. Plus, this exercise helps you to uncover your true calling and desires, through which upgrading your financial reality is activated. I recommend you complete the above exercise daily, because I know it works.

2. Create a list of yearly desires
After you practice your no-limits thinking, direct your attention to a year ahead. If everything was going perfectly for you and you simply could not fail, what would you want

to experience in the next 365 days? Consider how you want to give, grow and gain. Firstly, consider how you want to give to other people. Perhaps it will make your heart full if you take your friends out to dinner, or your family on a wonderful holiday. Perhaps, you want to donate generously to your favourite charity, or give your loved one an unexpected gift. Be as specific as you can be. Secondly, think about how you want to grow during this period or how you want your business to grow. Perhaps, you want to invest in hiring a new member of staff, increase your advertising budget, or invest in a coaching or educational programme. Write all these points down. Thirdly, consider what you want to gain.

Here, we are talking about your earthly, physical desires. These are important too and it is important to pay attention to them in balance and in relation to giving and growing. In my experience, many women put themselves last and that simply cannot be when you want to upgrade your financial reality! So, write down everything you want to gain personally during the next year. Perhaps you want to shop for new clothes, take a wonderful vacation, buy yourself something beautiful. Whatever it is, write your list down. Once you are finished with your list of intentions, go through it again. Does your list include any 'shoulds'? You know, those things you want out of obligation? How about those things that would be nice to do/have, but you don't really, really desire them? Tidy up your list and make sure it includes everything—but no more—than what you truly desire to create during the next year.

3. Turn concepts into feelings, extraordinary into ordinary
Be very specific; for example never say, 'One of my intentions for next year is to expand my property portfolio.' This is a very vague goal that sits in your head as a concept

only. Instead, surround yourself with people who are property investors. Go to those type of meetings where acquiring properties is in everyone's mind. Understand their way of thinking. Decide what type of properties you want to own, and what are the first steps towards making that happen. Do the same with all of your other big intentions and goals. If you want, for example, to take your family for luxury holidays, research destinations, hotels, travel etc. and find out how much money you specifically need. Make all of your intentions tangible, specific and emotionally highly desirable.

4. Set non-negotiable monthly intentions
Now, direct your focus to the next 30 days. Which of these yearly intentions are you going to make happen? Make a list and make sure your giving, growing, and gaining energies are in balance. Make sure you make that list easily accessible, so you can revisit it every day. This is how you are going to expand during the next 30 days and you are going to help the universe to expand with it. Remember, the universe is expanding and experiencing itself through your eyes, ears and hands. It wants what you want for you more than you want it; what you seek is seeking you.

5. Calculate your perfect monthly money intention; and a unique money mantra
Assign a money figure to each monthly intention. Add them all up. Then, add to this number your responsibilities, both personal and business. For example, mortgage, salaries and payable taxes, etc. You will come up with a specific money goal that is perfect for you right now. Then, create your unique money mantra, for example, 'I am easily receiving x amount of money or more, right now.' Put this mantra

everywhere you can; on your mirror, in your purse, on your office desk, and on your computer screen. You can also turn this mantra into a question, 'Why am I receiving x amount of money or more, right now with ease?'

This kind of mantra or question will direct your mind's focus in the right way. You are not saying to yourself, 'I have x amount of money.' This type of specific statement can often make you feel like you are lying to yourself and your brain will reject that. Specific statements about what you have—while you don't have it—can also evoke the sense of lack and that is exactly the energy you will emanate. So, you will get more of it. Instead, by focusing on, 'Why am I receiving x amount of money right now, with ease?' you are focusing on the process of receiving. You are acknowledging that you cannot perceive the working of this intelligent universe via your physical senses alone. But in fact, the entire universe is working for you right now, in this red hot minute and it is reorganising itself to meet your intention for expansion. Keep this mantra/question on the top of your mind throughout the month and repeat it often.

6. Create your action plan
Of course, your body is a conduit via which you receive financial abundance, but action is essential. It is important, however, to acknowledge that your physical you is only part of the creation here. Thinking that you and only you need to work very hard making money is practicing By Me Consciousness and can make you feel exhausted very quickly. Approach your action planning from Through Me and As Me Consciousness. This is why I love Mike Dooley's *The Triangle Approach* to creating a plan of action for achieving any specific goal, as he describes in his book, *Leveraging the Universe and Engaging Life's Magic.* Draw a large triangle and

divide it into two columns, so you will have a left and right side for the triangle. Write your unique monthly money mantra on the top of the triangle and label the left side of the triangle with 'Me' and the right side with 'The Universe'. On your side of the triangle, write down all the things you can do—physically, logically and spiritually—to achieve your goal. On the other side of the triangle—the right side of the triangle—write down all the ways you want the universe to support you in achieving your goal.

These might include:
- Put soul-aligned clients in my path
- Provide me with inspired ideas for achieving this goal with ease
- Turn my insecurities, doubts and fears into excitement
- Arrange circumstances to achieve my goal with ease.

Once you have finished, focus your attention on completing your part of the deal—completing actions on the left side of the triangle—knowing that the bigger side of you—the entire universe—is engaged in this process too, supporting you every step of the way.

Step Three: Align your money beliefs with your growth intentions

Everyone has a story about money. Generally, it is about our unconscious beliefs about money, and how they translate into our relationship with mone; money patterns, and everyday money experiences. If you want to upgrade your financial reality, it is essential you upgrade your beliefs and assumptions about money too. It is time to change your money story, so to speak.

177

For example, I grew up in an entrepreneurial family. My father owned a building complex with several shops and bars. We were living in a nice house and on the surface I grew up with a silver spoon in my mouth. However, my father didn't manage money wisely. I repetitively witnessed my mother desperately trying to find the money to pay the next bill or supplier. She worried about money all the time and that made me feel very insecure. This helped me to develop my own unhealthy assumptions about money, which are listed below as examples which might resonate with you.

- You need to work very hard for money.
- Money doesn't grow on trees.
- You are never safe.
- When money appears, it goes away very quickly.
- There is money around you, but you cannot have any of it.
- Wealth is for someone else.
- Having money will make you irresponsible.
- No matter how much money you make, it is never enough.

I carried many of these beliefs into my adult life without knowing it. I always worked hard and as my salary grew, so did my money worries. I always managed to create a sort of drama—unexpected bills, accidents and family emergencies etc.—so I could never hold on to any money and this reaffirmed my pattern, 'No matter how much money you make, it is never enough'. Revisiting my money stories and changing my embedded assumptions about money was an important step to create extraordinary growth in my business. I continue to do so with each calling for financial and business up-levelling. And so it will be in your case, my darling.

It is time to acknowledge which money beliefs you adopted during your life and change those that are not aligned with your extraordinary growth. We adopt most of our beliefs in our childhood—before the age of seven, in the imprint period—but we continue to form our relationship with money until our early thirties. However, it is never too late—or too early—to become aware of our money beliefs and do something about them. Simply acknowledging that our beliefs around money are not set in stone, is often enough to start shifting our money story.

> *'Beliefs are not true. They are constructs*
> *around which we organise our behaviours.*
> *So, we each behave as though our beliefs were true.*
> *And for this reason all our beliefs come true,*
> *for beliefs, whether empowering or limiting,*
> *are self-fulfilling prophecies.'*
>
> *Sue Knight*

1. Acknowledge your limiting beliefs about money

The first step in your money belief overhaul is to simply acknowledge what assumptions about money are limiting you. One of the ways you can do this is to observe your self-talk about money during a period of several days. Here are a few common negative beliefs about money. As you are reading through the list, please avoid adopting them as your own. Instead, see if any of them resonate with you.

- There isn't enough: belief in scarcity.
- I have to work hard for money.
- Money is the root of all evil.
- It is hard to keep money.
- Money is not that important.

- Making money means that I am taking it from someone else.
- Money doesn't grow on trees.
- Only manipulative people can be rich.
- You shouldn't make a lot of money by helping people.
- My work is easy, it is wrong to make a lot of money by doing something easy.
- We should be satisfied with what we have and not be greedy.
- Life/fuel/education is too expensive.
- I am not good with money.
- My family has never been rich.
- Money is a limited resource.
- I can be either rich or happy/healthy/loved etc.

Make your own list of money beliefs that no longer serve you.

2. Insert doubt
To rewrite these beliefs on a neurological level, the first thing you want to do is to insert doubt into them. With each set of beliefs that are not aligned with your extraordinary growth, ask yourself, 'Why might this not be true?' Write down as many reasons as you can think of.

3. Choose a new perspective
It is up to you to develop a new belief, and you can do that through finding a new, healthier perspective. With each of your limiting money beliefs, ask yourself, 'How does my higher-self see this?' The other question that will guide you to develop a new perspective is, 'Why might the opposite be true?' We can only experience negative emotions associated with limiting beliefs and circumstances that we create as a result of them, because we are not seeing things

from a higher perspective. We are buying into limited, ego-based thinking.

For example, if one of your limiting beliefs is that you cannot be incredibly rich and loved or liked at the same time, you will want to acknowledge that money cannot possibly change your character. Corrupt people will become more corrupt with more money while generous people will become more generous with more money and so on. It is entirely possible that you will be even more loved when you have more money, because it will allow you to express yourself in your fullness. Some people will stop liking you for that. They probably aren't a perfect energetic match for you anyway and there will be always more people who will appreciate you than not appreciate you.

The chances are that you are already familiar with the importance of working on your belief system, but I don't want you to skip this step because you have 'been there, done that'. The fact is, if you are not living the financial reality you want, you are running a money pattern that is not healthy for you. This money pattern can be easily addressed through realising the limiting assumptions that created that pattern and that is what this exercise is about.

Shifting even one limiting money belief can make a profound difference for you. For example, Michala Leyland, owner of Wood For The Trees Coaching, worked in the charity sector for many years prior to starting her coaching business. Unfortunately, she carried one of the beliefs developed during these years into her business; that she always had to find the resources for her clients for them to be able to access her services. You can imagine how limiting this way of thinking was. Once she recognised and shifted that belief she was able to double her coaching fees with ease, promoting healthy growth in her business.

In another example, my client Isobel thought that making money important makes you a bad person. Once she recognised that you can make money one of your priorities and be a good person—and you can maintain your highest integrity—she was able to set and subsequently achieve, a highly ambitious money goal. I could write a whole book about the many true examples of how shifting one limiting belief can profoundly affect your thinking and shape your financial reality. But the point is simple. Every time you want to upgrade your financial reality, you need to upgrade your beliefs about money.

Step Four: Increase the flow of money

How would it feel if money flowed to you at three times, four times, five times the current rate? Probably pretty fabulous, right? Now, it is up to us how much of this flow we experience. Energetically speaking, money is limitless, like an ever-flowing river, available to us at all times. But we also have the ability to slow down, or stop the flow, through our: assumptions about money; attitudes about money; feelings about money; and our money habits. When you have already completed the processes in the previous three steps, now you are in a perfect position to increase this flow. Here are a few processes to help you do exactly that. Several of them are internal processes while others require physical action, which is—as always—the best mindset work on the planet.

1. Internal spending
Check your bank balances and work out how much money you have available in this minute. Include your savings and optionally, your money availability through overdraft or credit cards. Now, you are going to spend this money—virtually—

20 times. You can do this in writing or in your mind only, but the important thing is that you emotionally feel the pleasure/relief/joy—or any other associated positive emotion—with each transaction. What do you want to purchase or pay for? What can you afford with the money you have? Imagine doing exactly that, again and again, until you have exhausted your balance. Then, do it 19 more times.

Doing this exercise is beneficial in several ways. Firstly, it will give you the feeling of choice. You see, we often say to ourselves, 'I can't afford this' whereas what is really happening is that we choose to hold on to money and use it differently, be it for bills or other, seemingly more urgent responsibilities. Completing this exercise will help you realise that if you really wanted, you could afford a lot more than you currently believe. The energy of choice is the energy of abundance, and that is the default state you want to be in to invite more money to flow into your experience.

Secondly, by virtually spending money repetitively you are practicing the energy of trust. You practice knowing that every time you spend, the money is replenished. While this is only a virtual game, it can have a profound effect on how you feel about spending money. You see, the need to hold on to money for safety sake is energy that directly contradicts the energy of abundance and flow, so if you tend to be tight with money because of fear, this is a money habit you will definitely want to address. This virtual spending process will help you reframe that belief.

2. Pay the bill
'Pay the bill' is a metaphor for paying for something that you have been meaning to buy; you have money to buy it, but you are postponing buying it because of lingering fear. It can be an outstanding bill, or something else, such as a piece of

jewellery you have been meaning to buy. Pay the bill, whatever it means to you. Increasing the flow of money is about expanding your capacity to spend with ease and receive with ease. If you are feeling negative emotions when you spend money that is exactly the energy that will be reflected back at you. Learn to spend your money knowing that the river of abundance is limitless and the more money you spend, the more you will receive.

I insert a word of caution here. I am not advising anyone to wipe out their bank accounts and pay for all their outstanding bills or desires at once. That would be foolish and irresponsible. You can practice the energy of ease while spending by taking small, systematic, responsible and empowering steps in that direction. It is all about transforming—step by step—the fear about spending money into the recognition of infinite abundance available to you.

I remember a few years ago, when I had my eyes on new bedroom furniture worth several thousand pounds. For months, I told myself, 'I will buy this when…' It took me a long time to recognise that whatever came after when—and there were many 'whens'—they were only excuses to cover up my fears about spending that amount of money on something nice, but not necessarily needed. I had money available for that furniture, I didn't have to steal or borrow to buy it. And yet I was procrastinating about spending that money for fear of running out of money. That is when I played a virtual spending game to start with and then went and bought that furniture. As if by miracle, I made exactly the same amount of money the very next day: except that these types of miracles are not miracles at all—it is the universe responding to your changed energy—the energy of trust, ease and abundance. This is exactly how this process— Pay the Bill—will help you to expand.

Perhaps the most joyous and expansive way of applying the Pay the Bill principle is to give some money away. Can you tip more than you are used to doing? Can you insert a few coins into shopping trollies in your local supermarket and pleasantly surprise the next shopper? Can you give a musician on the street a note, instead of a coin? The point is you cannot give that which you don't have and every time you give, you give it to yourself, tenfold. The energy of giving invites receiving. But, you cannot give with the expectation of gaining back; that is practicing the energy of lack. Give because it makes you feel good. The universe will reward you richly for it.

3. Track your money

If your money matters are not in order, address that right away. Hire the best bookkeepers and accountants in town. Money loves responsibility and it will thank you for treating it with respect. Never rely solely on your accountants to keep an eye on how your money is doing. Track it yourself.

'Whatever gets measured gets improved.'

Legendary management consultant Peter Drucker famously proclaimed this more than 40 years ago, and it continues to be true today. This is not true only from a practical perspective, but it is the energetic principle of, 'What you focus on, expands'. So, track, at a minimum, your weekly money areas you wish to improve. If you wish to wipe out your debt faster, track the amount of your debt weekly. If you wish to improve sales, track your sales. If you wish to improve your profitability, track your profitability. Engaging in tracking your money regularly—I suggest once a week at least—can cut the time between where you are money wise and where you want to be—by an enormous amount.

Rosie did exactly that, because she had accumulated more than £100K in debt; and according to her payment plan it was going to take her many years to pay it off. She decided to track the debt amount weekly and pay it off as quickly as possible. Seeing the amount of money owed every week and seeing it decreasing little by little, gave her the motivation to stay focused on money making activities and paying it off. By weekly tracking her money, she increased sales in her company tenfold and paid off her debt 24 years ahead of schedule!

4. Re-define the way you save

'Save for a rainy day!' is well-meaning advice, which many of us heard from our parents and grandparents and we took it to heart. However, I want you to consider, for a moment, what energy lies behind 'saving for a rainy day'. You will probably acknowledge that it is a fear, which is not the best energy to have when it comes to increasing the flow of money in your business and life. Am I suggesting that you stop saving? Of course not! But you may want to re-define the reason why you save. Stop saving for emergencies which will only energetically invite those emergencies to transpire in your real life. Instead, save for something expanding and life giving. For example, my savings account is called a Freedom Account and I regularly save money in that account, knowing that when I ever choose to stop working for a prolonged period of time, I can do that. The point is that this works and when you give a positive purpose to your savings, it may motivate you to save more!

5. Practice gratitude

Not enough words can express the power of gratitude. It is

the most healing and creative emotion of all. When we are truly grateful for what we have, we are tuning into the vibration of abundance and we are priming ourselves for noticing and creating more of the things that give us that exact feeling. Take stock of everything you are grateful for in your life. Write down, or mentally list, all the things you have, expressing a deep gratitude for each of them. Allow yourself to feel gratitude for each of these things in fullness. Remember to include all those things you usually take for granted. Imagine for a moment, what it would be like without hot water, electricity or the Internet! Include all the things you also wish to have tomorrow. This is bound to evoke a feeling of richness in you and that is exactly what you want to foster when upgrading your financial reality.

The next level of money abundance in your business is nothing more or nothing less than your state of mind. You have got to feel rich to invite more money to flow through your experience. It is not the other way round. It is only when you feel rich that you can receive ideas for making the next level of your income. It is only then that the universe will be able to grant you the right circumstances for your next level of income. It is then that you find yourself at the right place, in the right time, receiving with ease and seeing the journey of your extraordinary growth unfolding perfectly, rather than having to push for it every day. We all know about the power of gratitude, but we can easily forget about it because of our busy-ness.

Sometimes it is the simplest things, that are easily missed, that make the biggest difference. And gratitude is definitely one of those aspects of life. You might choose to expand the practice of gratitude into your money matters too. Practice feeling grateful when checking your money and tracking your money. Instead of focusing on how much money you currently have, give thanks for all the financial abundance that has already flowed through you during the last month, three months, last year, or last ten years. When you list all the growth, pleasure, comfort and joy that you have experienced as a result of the money you have already received, you cannot help but feel incredibly abundant and grateful. Apply the same feeling to your bills. For example, you can be pissed off that you have another large electricity bill to pay; or you can give thanks for the comfort and warmth you have been able to experience as a result of using electricity. Gratitude has the power to transform all your fears about money into ever expanding abundance. Use it often.

EXTRAORDINARY GROWTH CHALLENGE: THE 30 DAY MONEY UPGRADE

In this chapter, you have been introduced to 17 money upgrade processes, which fall into four steps for upgrading your money consciousness.

1. Take control of your money.
2. Set powerful money intentions.
3. Align your money beliefs with your growth intentions.
4. Increase the flow of money.

These processes will work, and make you a direct channel to insane amounts of clients and money when you apply them. Thus, I challenge you, no matter where you are right now, to play with these processes during the next 30 days. Spend a little time on these money upgrade processes every day. You can take them one by one, or complete those that call you the most. The most important aspect is to give yourself at least 30 days where you pay attention to your relationship with money and you improve it. When you upgrade how you apply your personal energy around the subject of money, your entire business will upgrade too, and that is exactly why you are reading this, right?

IN THIS CHAPTER YOU HAVE DISCOVERED

- The importance of upgrading your money consciousness when creating the next level of growth in your business.
- The four-step formula for upgrading your money consciousness.
- Seventeen processes to help you energetically align yourself with extraordinary growth and an abundance of money flowing through your business.

Before you move onto the next chapter, ask yourself the following questions and write down your answers to help you on your extraordinary growth journey.

1. If all my current circumstances are a direct result of my beliefs, what beliefs do I want to change?
2. What does money mean to me?
3. How do I want to improve my relationship with money?

In the next chapter, we will make sure you are able to charge what your service is truly worth; and with that, empower yourself, your business, and your clients—big time.

10
LEAP INTO CHARGING HIGH-END FEES

AND FEEL GREAT ABOUT IT

*'You have the right and duty to live at your highest level,
serve at your highest level, and charge accordingly.'*

I HAD COMPLETED four days of executive training and coaching with a new client. It was a big project for me, because he was the Senior Vice President of one of the largest financial institutions in the world, and he had given me plenty of positive feedback throughout. I knew he had greatly benefitted from the programme, but I needed a professional review.

I asked, 'Please be honest; what could I have done better?' John went—for a moment—into thinking mode and then replied, 'Honestly? You surpassed my expectations by 1000%. I would go as far as to say that this was the best programme I have taken so far; and I have two master degrees and I invest heavily in my development. But there is one thing I would like to give you constructive feedback about. Are you open to that?' I felt myself sinking into the chair as I said, 'Yes, of course.' He continued, 'Your pricing. From what you charged, I would never have assumed you were such a great trainer and coach, and if it were not for a

190

fantastic recommendation from my colleague, I would never have gone for coaching that was so cheap.' I sank still further into my chair. I felt that I was experiencing one of the most embarrassing moments of my life.

My mind raced to our initial conversation on the telephone, when John had booked his programme with me. We had immediately established a great rapport and I knew he was a great fit for what I had to offer, but when it came to the part of the conversation about the investment fee, I hesitated. It was during the time when I was struggling with the aftermath of losing my first business. I was grateful for any business that came my way, let alone from a board level executive of a blue-chip company, so I offered him a price that would cause 'no resistance'. Clearly, I had undercharged myself and if it were not for a warm recommendation from one of his colleagues, it would have cost me the deal and a good friend.

Now, it has been several years since that embarrassing moment; and I would like to say that since then I have never, ever undercharged for my services again; but that would be a lie. I continued to do so, until I understood with every fibre of my being that undercharging for my 1-2-1 services was not only hurting my business, but my clients as well. Gradually, I increased my 1-2-1 fees tenfold. The more I learned to trust my expertise and the creative power of my clients, the easier it became to attract those high-end clients and grow my business effortlessly. And that is what we are going to do in this chapter, my darling. We are going to make sure you are deeply in touch with the tremendous benefits of claiming your worth and charging high-end fees for your services. If you have a sense that you undercharge yourself, or that you have a room to grow your price banding, we are going to address that today.

191

You may be wondering: what is considered as high-end? Unfortunately, this cannot be defined in any exact number because it is subjective to you, your business and your audience. For many people, high-end services might start at £5K upwards, for other people it may be £10K, £20K or £100K and upwards. In the coaching industry, for example, there are three standard pricing structures.

1. Hourly: you charge an hourly rate for each hour of your coaching.
2. Packages: you bundle your coaching sessions and offer a certain number to solve your client's problem, and charge for the package total.
3. High-end/premium: you don't price your coaching services based on the amount of coaching hours provided, but rather on the value and Return On Investment, which your client receives.

Now, there is nothing wrong with charging hourly fees, or packages of sessions. But the truth is, these two pricing structures put limits on your earning potential. You will never be able to step away from your business for a long period of time and know your business is thriving anyway; and—if you are not careful—charging an hourly rate can lead to exhaustion. It happened to one of my gorgeous friends, Anjali and it wasn't nice. As an extremely talented intuitive therapist, she had never suffered from a lack of clients, in fact the opposite. Business executives, doctors and scientists alike flocked into her therapy room near central London to solve their most pressing problems, often leaving Anjali with a three-month waiting list. In addition, she used a sliding scale pricing range for her therapy to help those people most in need.

This meant that Anjal worked from morning until the late hours in the evening, day in and day out. 'I'm fine! I love my work and I love helping other people!' was Anjali's response whenever I, or any of her friends expressed concern about the pace of her work. Yes, Anjali was fine. Until one day, when she fell flat on her face out of exhaustion, smashing her front teeth. As you can imagine, the long and painful recovery forced her to re-evaluate the way she worked and the way she valued the incredible value she provided her clients.

At other times, undercharging for our services can lead us to metaphorically fall flat on our face. Time and time again, I have heard from talented women coaches about how they are thinking of giving up because their clients are: not showing up for sessions; or they are not following up on the agreed tasks; or they need hours upon hours of attention outside of the paid coaching hours; leaving these women coaches often feeling resentful—or worse— doubting the quality of their work. Choosing to charge high-end fees puts a stop to all of that. But of course, it is not for everyone. High-end fees or increasing your fees substantially demands delivering a high quality of work. Plus, women who choose this path choose the path of internal growth because your fees can never overgrow the woman you are on the inside.

Naturally, each increase in fees, let alone transitioning from charging an hourly rate to charging high-end fees, can awaken our dear ego. But saying the following will not help you either: 'Nobody will hire me when I increase my pricing. People will consider me selfish and greedy. Charging high-end makes me feel a fraud.' If you have been feeling you are not charging your worth and it is time to increase your fees substantially—or to transition to high-end fees instead of an hourly/package pricing model—here are five things you need to remind yourself. They will help to quieten your ego and align it with your extraordinary growth; charge appropriately; and serve at your highest level, allowing your business to grow and thrive like never before.

Your value cannot be measured in time

There is a famous story about a woman who once saw Picasso doodle on a napkin in a restaurant. She went across to his table and asked him how much she would have to pay to have that napkin. He said, '20,000 US dollars. 'She replied, 'What? It only took you five minutes to draw it!' His answer was, 'No, madam, it took me my whole life.'

The same goes for you. As a coach or expert in your field you are helping your clients to draw a new life on their canvas. You are not bringing only your time to your coaching sessions. You are bringing all your life experiences, your education and your training. You are bringing all the books you have read and all the professional development courses you have invested in. You are bringing all your past mistakes and what you have learned from them. In addition, you are bringing all your extensive skills and expertise. Your value—and what you should charge—simply cannot be measured in time. It is way more than the time you spend with your clients! The only correct way to set your fees is to base them on the value your clients receive as a result of hiring you. Consider what is the final outcome of your service for your clients and what value it will bring to their lives and work, emotionally, financially, physically and spiritually.

I recall a client who went through a very bitter divorce and as a result, suffered from low self-esteem and anxiety.

She said, 'I was willing to do anything to relieve the pain I was in, even to sell my house, if it came to it!' Eventually, she found a coach who guided her to adopt new ways of thinking and re-create her life. In time, she concluded, 'Even though the fee was steep, it was the best investment I have ever made in myself, and 100% worth it.'

You see, the value this client reaped from hiring a professional was priceless and this should be the case with your paying clients too. Beyond the value of your service, there are only two other questions you need to ask yourself when considering the optimal pricing for your offerings.

1. What does my ideal client need to invest, to guarantee their absolute commitment to the process?
Since that embarrassing moment in John's office, I have invested more than six figures into my development. Many of the investments I have made felt comfortable, but others have seriously not been! I will let you guess which type of investment I worked harder for, to make the investment worth it. Of course, it was with those fees that stretched me. The equation is simple. The more you charge, the more your clients value your service and the more energy, commitment and focus, your client will put into making the process work. The same goes for you as their service provider. For your client to achieve the results they want, there needs to be the right energy exchange and that is exactly what high-end fees are all about. Remember, your fees should make your prospective clients a little uncomfortable. You don't want to serve clients who will say to themselves, 'I'll try this, I have nothing to lose!'
2. How much do I need to be paid to be valued?
The fees you charge for your personal work with clients is

not your personal salary. Consider what is the cost of delivering your service; your personal time; travel expenses; administration support; and software management etc. It is important that what you are paid at the end of all the expenses outlay, will make you feel valued otherwise you won't be able to bring your best energy and focus to your work. Plus, you need to consider dedicating a certain percentage of your fees to fuelling the growth of your business because treating your business as a piggy bank is the fastest way to stagnation and ultimately, disintegration.

It takes less energy to serve a few high-value clients than a ton of low-end clients

The chances are you started your business because you want to make a positive difference in the lives of other people and you want to be generously paid for it. You may have experienced—or are experiencing—trying to achieve this by competing on price for your services. But here is the thing: going down this route and earning your place in the marketplace is a very hard road to travel. You see, you need to sell a ton of low-end products to be sufficiently profitable to live the freedom you desire and allow your business to grow the way you want and that takes energy and lots of it. In fact, it can be far easier to sell a few high-value products rather than plenty of low-value products.

Let's say you absolutely had to make one million pounds in revenues during the next 12 months. You don't have a huge network or the influencer status yet. What is going to be more achievable: selling 10,000 products at £100, or serving 40 clients through a £25,000 offering? Most people would choose the second option, and rightfully so. It takes far less doing to attract 40 of your most perfect, soul-aligned clients, rather than selling a ton of low-end products. However, there is always a place and time for low-end offerings. But I wholeheartedly believe this decision should be made consciously, strategically and in alignment with your personality.

Many change-makers are lighthouses. They see themselves on big stages, serving millions of people and shining their light, so to speak. Other change-makers are influencer's influencers who are not driven by being the centre of the stage, or working with masses, but rather, they choose to work with a few key individuals, but on a high-level, which one are you; a lighthouse or an influencer's influencer? If you are the influencer's influencer, offering low-end products will give you nothing more than plenty of headaches. Simply don't go there. Instead, work on positioning yourself as an expert for experts and charge accordingly.

If you are a lighthouse, you will naturally be drawn to offering products that can serve many people. This is great and I recommend you include high-end offerings, especially before you make your millions and serve millions. Why, because it doesn't take a ton of effort to attract and serve a few high-end clients per month, although it does require personal mastery and alignment. Then, you can use part of the—hopefully substantial—profits, to build an eco-system in your business that will allow you to serve masses.

Sarah Morgan, author of *Welcome To The Beginning Of Everything You Want*, is a perfect example of how serving at your highest level can move your business upwards in leaps and bounds. After working for many years in the

Public Relations industry, she decided to follow her intuition and start a business as a manifesting coach. Sarah is one of those women who deliver energetic marketing completely naturally. Her energy is magnetic, her vision is bigger than life and she is a walking example of manifesting the things she wants with ease. She quickly attracted followers from all across the globe and sold plenty of low-end programmes.

There was one catch though. She wasn't making sufficient profits to grow her influence the way she wanted. She desired to quantum leap her business to the next level and ideally, fast. She joined my VIP Mastermind and to start with we streamlined Sarah's offerings and she immediately stopped offering those programmes she wasn't utterly in love with. Secondly, we worked on Sarah's strategy and energy, so she could start offering high-end products and that she did. Within two months, she created and sold a £10K group programme, which meant she created space and money to write two books on her subject, as well as implement structures in her business that allowed her to grow her business much faster.

Sarah's feedback was, 'This work was not easy at times. To be able to serve high-value clients, I had to make several uncomfortable decisions and on a few occasions, my ego had a really good field day. But it also completely revolutionised my business and massively expanded it.' Whether you are a lighthouse like Sarah, or an influencer's influencer, focusing on your high-value clients and serving at your highest level is the surest way to create extraordinary growth in your business.

There is an abundance of clients you are meant to serve, at whatever fees

198

A word of warning; be careful about who and what you listen to and take on board when it comes to marketing and selling. Sometimes you may come across advice such as this. 'The popular advice you may be hearing is that marketing online is the best way to chase clients all across the world and so naturally that is what most business owners are trying to do. Yet, the more fishermen there are in that ocean, the less fish there are for everyone to catch. When you are trying to fish for clients in the global ocean it is not as easy to succeed, because other people with bigger businesses are like these big ocean liners; and they have these big expensive nets, and they are casting them. They are the ones who are scooping up all the clients and leaving you the leftovers.'

When I read this advice for the first time, it left me feeling really furious because if I had listened to such 'sound marketing advice' when I was contemplating taking my business online with a view to serving high-end clients globally, I would have never taken that step. I would never have gathered the courage to go from offline networking to building a global presence online. You see I truly believe the way we view our chances of succeeding is a matter of perspective.

Sure, you can focus on competition and create a strategy about how you are going to claim your slice of a pie in the marketplace. Or, you can consider the vastness of this energetic universe and acknowledge that you are creating your own marketplace. You can assume you are going against the big players who have already eaten the bigger slice of the pie, leaving you with the leftovers. Or you can acknowledge that there is nobody else exactly like you, that you are a completely unique conduit of the universal wisdom and you have as much opportunity to succeed as any other expert. You can choose to believe that we are here to chase clients, fish for clients, scoop clients and compete with other people for clients, or, you can choose to attract perfect-for-you clients. Since clients are nothing more or nothing less than a reflection of your consciousness, you are in charge of choosing which consciousness you adopt; what kind of clients you want to serve; and how you want to serve them.

From an energetic perspective, it is impossible to run out of clients, given you have a genuine calling to serve because that calling itself is a confirmation that there are more than enough clients to satisfy your calling. Remember, the universe shows you how it wants to express itself through you via your desire. It is a strong physical signal that calls you upwards.

Read this again, please, because this is very important. Your calling to serve high-value clients is all the confirmation you need that there are more than enough clients available to you, right now. You have got to believe this, otherwise you can slip into Lack Consciousness and that surely doesn't create ripples and growth. Plus, we don't need to go into the metaphysics to be able to realise that there are plenty of clients for us, each and every one of us, at whatever level.

Consider this. There are seven and a half billion people living on this planet right now. If you wanted to count us all, it would take you more than 237 and half years, without taking breaks for sleeping, drinking or eating. That is how big that number is. Sure, not all of those people are your ideal clients. But the truth is that leaves you with at least 7,500 one-in-a-million-clients. Think about this: clients who are a perfect match to your energetic blueprint and your expertise, will happily pay you £5k, £10k, £20k, £50k, or whatever £K for your best work. Can you serve 7,500 clients through your high-value offerings right now? Probably not, so be picky. Decide who that one-in-a-million client of yours is and organise your high-end offerings around them. This will revolutionise your business and take it in leaps and bounds forwards and upwards.

Your fees build trust with your clients or damage it

Here is the last point to consider on the importance of charging adequately. Your fees create a perception in your potential clients' minds about the quality of your work. The lower your prices are, the more risky your service is in your client's mind. Hence, charging only a little can be an instant credibility killer. Yes, learn from my embarrassing moment with John! Furthermore, low-paying clients refer more low-paying clients, and that is a cycle you certainly don't want to find yourself in.

My dear reader, you are a powerful woman and the chances are you worked for years to be able to bring your clients what you offer. Therefore you don't only have the right, but also the duty to charge our worth; to be valued and adequately compensated. You have the right and duty to assist your clients in the way they deserve to serve at your highest level and to do our best work with grace. If you are not charging what your expertise is worth, then let's go now—together—and change that today, right now!

The seven keys to creating irresistible high-value offerings

Of course, high-value offerings must be based on massive value. While I cannot tell you what exactly to include in your high-end offerings, since you are the expert, here are the seven keys to make your business offering irresistible to your ideal clients. You might want to use the list below as a checklist when you outline what specifically you want to offer to your audience. It will help you to communicate the value of your work with confidence and the energy of certainty; whether it is through your sales pages, marketing, or other parts of your sales process.

1. A compelling name with a big, bold and specific promise

What is the biggest result your offering can deliver? Make it plain to see. I started my online business with the launch of my *Get Fully Booked Academy* a high-end group programme, which was set up to help women coaches to become fully booked with their high-end, soul clients. The name of the programme was not the most original on the planet and yet, partially because there was no doubt what this course was about, it attracted hundreds of gorgeous clients from all around the world and helped them to build thriving coaching businesses. The big, bold promise is something your client will be able to imagine in their mind and it will evoke positive emotion when doing so. It will make them feel amazing when they imagine it. Get clear about what that is. Then, bring your big bold promise to the forefront of your selling and marketing.

2. Focus on benefits rather than process

As an expert, you know exactly what your clients need for them to get the results they want. For example, a relationship coach knows how self-love is extremely important on the journey to attracting the dream relationship. And yet, your potential clients who feels alone and dreams about being loved, probably doesn't go to bed crying themselves to sleep thinking, 'I wish I loved myself more'. The chances are, they don't give a damn about loving themselves at that point. They want to be loved. They want the other half who will give them that feeling. That is why an offering such as 'Attract Dream Love' will do always better than 'The Power of Self-Love'. Offer your clients what they truly want. Then, give them what they need, so they can get what they want.

3. Value outweighs real or perceived cost

Of course, your clients need to know that the benefits they will reap out of working with you will far exceed what they put into it, be that in terms of their money, time or energy. This is not going to happen by listing features about your offering. Generally speaking, your clients don't give a damn about whether your programme has eight or twelve modules, whether you will work with them for three months or six months, whether you have one or twenty juicy bonuses. What they care about is how those features will help them to get what they want. That is why it is important to link every single feature of your offering with a strong benefit statement for your client. For example, instead of saying, my *Become a Sales Superstar* coaching programme includes a welcome questionnaire; twelve private sessions; and email support in between sessions, explain the benefits they will receive, as below.

This is what is included:

- a welcome questionnaire, which will help you be clear about the gaps in your selling process and unhelpful thinking patterns about selling;
- twelve weekly private sessions where we address every obstacle that stands between you and achieving your

203

most ambitious sales targets; and

• email support in-between sessions, to enable you to have all your burning questions answered and take the most productive steps forward.

Can you see how the features expressed in this way build the value of your offering?

4. Centre on active buyers, with the outcome plain to see

Never try to persuade clients they need your service. Instead, focus on those clients who are ready to buy from you. Be clear on your ideal client's 'Oh shit!' point, as described in Chapter Six and include that in the packaging of your offering. Also, make sure the client will be able to see the contrast between where they are now and where they can be once they invest in you. For example, going back to the *Get Fully Booked Academy* example, I used the phrase, 'from overlooked to fully booked' in my marketing materials, because it clearly illustrated the contrast between the client's 'Oh shit!' point and where they wanted to be.

5. Minimise risk

Especially when your clients are paying big bucks for your services, they need to know their money is a wise investment. Provide social proof and guarantees where appropriate; plus the sense of certainty that will ooze out of your entire selling process will do wonders in this regard.

6. Create emotional connection and build credibility

There may be plenty of experts in your niche, but there is only one you with your unique story. Share it. Let your potential clients know how what you offer them helped you. Open your heart. Your prospective client will feel it and they will feel comfortable with you. For example, they might think, 'She is like me, she can understand me and I want to be where she is'. Remember, clients buy your energy, so no matter what, let it bath every bit of your sales process.

7. Packaging matches value and pricing

Just as you wouldn't sell a diamond ring wrapped in newspapers, you don't want to present your work via the cheapest solutions available. For example, no sales page is a far better option than a sales page that is—and looks—self-made. Visual presentation of your service should always match the value you are offering and the pricing you demand. However, wherever possible, leave this aspect to professionals.

> *'Extraordinary growth pushes you into the unknown, a notion that you may find very scary, or see it as the field of infinite possibilities.'*

Here is a little secret. Even when you do your work and become fully aware of the dangers of undercharging and the benefits of charging high-end fees for your clients and your business; even when you create the most phenomenal high-end offering that will revolutionise your client's model of the world even then, you may feel nervous about increasing your fees. And guess what? That is okay. Everything new can feel a little scary and in fact, your client should feel a little nervous too. Working with you in a high-end capacity should certainly not be as easy a decision for your client as getting—or not getting—another cup of coffee. It should put your clients a little out of their comfort zone.

That is how they will be able to create an immediate energetic shift once they invest in you. They will be inventing their wings in that moment, so to speak. A little nervousness is okay. It will disappear once you make those first few sales on the higher level and settle in this new energy. However, if that nervousness makes you hesitant about increasing your fees—even though you know it is way past the right time to do so—or it is a completely delimitating emotion, we can do something with that too. In fact, we can deal with it right away and turn that nervousness into absolute readiness, with this next extraordinary growth challenge.

EXTRAORDINARY GROWTH CHALLENGE: ENERGETIC ALIGNMENT WITH CHARGING HIGH-END FEES

This powerful and quick exercise will minimise—or even completely dissolve—your fears about increasing your fees and align your energy with charging the high-end fees you deserve. Complete this exercise after you outline your high-value offering and decide on how much you will charge for this service. You can do this exercise as a brief meditation, visualisation or complete it via journaling. The choice is yours.

Step One: Bring into your awareness the fee you want to charge. Notice how it makes you feel, give a name to that specific emotion. Perhaps it is fear, doubt, nervousness, or something else. Also, notice the intensity of this emotion from 0, where you feel nothing, to 10, where the negative emotion is extremely intense.

206

Step Two: Acknowledge that the version of you who charges this fee with confidence already exists vibrationally, in the field of pure potentiality. Then, acknowledge that there also exists the version of you that charges twice the fees you are planning to charge and you do so with confidence.

Step Three: Go there in your mind's eye. Tune into that version of you who charges twice more than you are planning to charge right now. Imagine you have plenty of enquiries about your services. Imagine having amazing sales conversations. Imagine stating this fee with complete confidence. Imagine your client responding with, 'Let's do it'. Imagine how much you will enjoy working with these clients and what phenomenal transformations and results they will acheive through working with you at this level.

Complete this exercise, to embed these principles by writing your answers to the following simple, but profound questions.
- What will it feel like when I am charging twice the fee I am planning to and with complete confidence and ease?
- What will it feel like when I have client after client saying Yes to my offerings?

Write down your answers in as much detail as you can, until all you can feel is pure positive emotion.

Step Four: Now ask yourself, How does it feel to charge the fees I am planning to? Where is your emotion on the scale of 0-10?

If you did not rush through this exercise you will find that your negative emotions about charging high-end fees will reduce dramatically, or disappear altogether. You may suddenly feel very confident about charging adequate high-end fees. This is because you vibrationally put yourself—even though briefly—into a much higher energetic level of consciousness. You created a contrast in your mind between the fees you want to charge and the fees that are twice as high. This is a perfect way to fool your ego and become aligned with charging high-end fees quickly. Of course, you might need to repeat this exercise again, but this can be a fast way to empower you to charge your worth.

This is exactly what happened to my client, Emily King, founder of the Rich Woman and an incredible coach based in Canada. During our first session she shared with me that she was currently charging a thousand dollars for her three month coaching programme and she wanted to increase her fees, but she did not feel confident enough. After we covered all the basics—including making sure that her clients would receive a substantial Return On Investment after investing in her new level of fees—Emily decided she wanted to charge $2.5K for her coaching. I guided Emily to do the exercise above during that session. '$2.5K feels like an absolute no-brainer,' she exclaimed when we finished. Following our business coaching call, Emily was scheduled to have a sales call with a potential client and guess what—she immediately sold her coaching package at this new fee, with complete ease.

During our four month coaching, Emily increased her fees several times, and became confident in charging $5K for her three month coaching package. This significantly improved the quality of clients she attracted, as well as her profitability.

The same can happen to you, my darling. And it does not matter whether you are called to offer a £5k, £10k or £50k service. The process is exactly the same. When you are amazing at what you do; have a passion for it; and love your clients, it is simply a matter of choice to leap to high-end fees and serve at your highest level. Your clients, your business, your loved ones and your soul will thank you for it.

IN THIS CHAPTER, YOU HAVE DISCOVERED

- The threats of undercharging for your services
- The tremendous benefits of charging high-end fees, for you and for your clients
- The difference between lighthouse and influencer's influencer personalities and how may this influence your marketing
- How to go from undercharging to charging your worth
- Leaping into charging high-end fees and serving at your highest level and becoming your highest level are a matter of your choice

Here are three reinforcement questions for you.
1. Are my current fees ensuring my clients are totally committed to getting the results they want?
2. Are my current fees attracting the type of clients I truly want to serve?
3. Are my current fees allowing me to invest in the growth of my business and live the lifestyle I desire?

If the answers to any of these questions for you is no, then you now know what to do about it, don't you my darling?

11
Extraordinary Growth

'Flow is not only a calm river. Rapids are also a form of flow and a sign of accelerated change and growth.'

'But how long will it take me to create the growth in my business I want?': this is the question that rests on many women's minds. After all, we are ambitious creatures, and yesterday may be a little too late. The only honest answer to this can only be, 'It depends'. You see each of our journeys is very different. We are different people, with different programming, different sizes of networks to start with, different sets of skills, different talents and gifts.

In a nutshell, the 'how long' question depends on the degree of change required and your willingness to focus on that which you want, rather than your ego. You will create the next quantum leap in your business; and the next one; and the next one after that; when you stop tolerating not having it. Having said that, there are things we can do to reduce the number of weeks, months and years between where you are now and where you desire to be. And that is what this final chapter is about; offering you the guidance to speed up the process of extraordinary growth without going into overwhelm.

210

First things first though: we want to be honest with ourselves. We want to be aware of the challenges we may come across and be prepared for them. You see, our logical minds want to think that our business will grow in exact proportion to our efforts. That is, however, seldom true. Most successful businesses go through the three critical stages—repetitively—of the S Curve.

The S Curve Process

The first stage of the business, represented by the bottom part of S, is commonly called the **Infancy Stage**. Everyone in business is very familiar with this exciting stage. You have the birth of your business idea; you conduct your market research, put together your business plan, perhaps commission someone to create your website and finally you launch your business. This doesn't necessarily mean that clients will start flocking to your doors right away. In this initial and exciting stage of business, we inevitably go through a steep learning curve.

We learn many things, and become aware of many other things we don't know we should know about. We need to learn how to harmonise various aspects of a successful business; our brand and positioning in the market; sales channels; marketing channels; and the structure of the business, while developing crucial skills for success in the business; from selling and marketing skills; through to learning various systems and developing ourselves as women, thinkers, and leaders.

It is during this time that our belief in our vision is tested the most. While you work very hard on bringing in the revenue and getting your brand known, often your results don't match your expectations. The avalanche of clients may seem nowhere in sight and at times, you may feel disappointed, full of worry and doubt.

Yet, given that you don't stop, you will inevitably hit a turning point in your business and enter the second, **Rapid Growth Stage**. Clients start pouring in. Your business is truly taking off and you feel a huge sense of satisfaction. But the chances are, you will also feel tired. This amount of business is well out of your comfort zone and you simply cannot do it all: delivering the work; looking after your clients; and everything else that keeps your business going. How prepared you are for this challenge, because how you respond to it is crucial. Ideally, you will be prepared for this stage well in advance and can implement your plan systematically and confidently. Who you hire, what you outsource, and how you systemise, are all activities that are far more fruitful when done in a pro-active, rather than reactive mode of thinking.

However, the rapid growth stage doesn't last forever. Inevitably, your business will stabilise, entering the third, **Maturity Stage**. You feel you have time to breath and enjoy the fruits of your efforts. And yet the decisions you make— or don't make—in this stage of your business, will profoundly affect its future. You see, maturity represents the comfort zone and it cannot last forever. You either innovate and develop new products and services for your clients, or expand to new markets, essentially re-entering stage one— the Infancy Stage—of the next level of your business, or you risk future decline. The moment you enter the Maturity Stage of your business, or well before that, the question on your mind should be, 'What is the next S-curve I am going to embark on?' Your business simply needs to move quicker than the world around it.

The three stages of creating quantum leaps

Similarly, there are three stages of creating extraordinary growth from the energetic perspective.

1. Intention
2. Bridging
3. Manifestation

First, we set powerful **intentions** for growth. We make a non-negotiable decision. This is where we tap into a potential reality, revealed to us by our higher-self, and accept it as ours. In that moment, the universe will start re-arranging itself to satisfy your new preference.

The third stage is the one we all want; **manifestation**, when things in front of us are exactly as we envisioned them, or even better. It is the transitional stage in-between that can challenge us or even—if not prepared—stop us all together: **bridging**.

This is the bridge between your old and new reality, a space that will—given you set intentions for extraordinary growth—most certainly put you out of your comfort zone. And what you do while walking on that bridge can make the difference between reaching the other side—the business of your dreams—with grace, or falling flat on your face. I want you to succeed. If you have big dreams, it is your right to live those dreams. It is your destiny. So, my dear reader, here are four challenges you may meet on your way from the old to the new and how to deal with them gracefully.

1. Follow the butterflies

You decide to make that phone call. Approach that person. Step on that stage. Shoot that video. Run that webinar. Follow up. Take that next step towards your extraordinary growth. And just before you make that step, your tummy is full of butterflies. You are scared. However, this is good. Those butterflies are showing you the signs towards the other side of the bridge. They are showing you that you are growing in this moment. Follow those butterflies, always. Next time, you will be less scared and after a while, you will realise that what used to scare you so much, is now your new normal. This is because you have changed. You have arrived at your next level of growth!

2. Negotiate with your ego

You decide to launch your new service, expand your team, or register for that high-level programme. You feel inspired to do this and you know this is your way to your next greatness. And then you sleep on it, and your ego awakens. She might scream at you, 'Who am I to think I can do this? I can't possibly pull this off. What was I thinking? I can't afford it, I don't have enough time for this!' Remember, your ego wants to keep you safe and it will use whatever tools necessary to trick you and keep you where you are. Sometimes, it will throw at you your old limitations, which you thought you had dealt with years ago. Other times, it will hit you with logic.

The more you grow, the more sophisticated your ego grows, and—as always—it is essential to recognise it for what it is. Your ego is a trickster. Never shut it up, let your ego speak. Let it offload. But, for heaven's sake, never identify with what your ego throws at you as your truth. Challenge it. Acknowledge that no matter how true something appears, it is always, always, only one of many options. Challenge your ego. Negotiate with your ego. If necessary, consider the worst outcome possible in detail and reassure yourself you are safe. Then, tell your ego to go to your pocket and join you for an exhilarating ride. At times, your ego thoughts can get really loud. But that doesn't matter. As long as you listen and you learn to move forward anyway, your ego won't be able to shout forever. Action aligned with your extraordinary growth is the fastest way to shun your ego. Use it.

3. Turn overwhelm into growth

Giving birth to the next level of business and life will take some pushing, pulling and energy that can move mountains. It can get overwhelming at times—both with the degree of change and to take the actions required—leaving you feeling that you cannot possibly do it all.

> *"Sure, you cannot do it all, but you can*
> *certainly have it all."*

Pay attention to support systems and people in your business at every stage, so you can spend as much time as possible in your zone of genius, money, and client generating activities. Nic Rixon, renowned United Kingdom strategist who has helped numerous businesses scale up beyond seven and eight figure-a-year revenues, divides activities, people, and systems into three crucial categories.

Blue Category: everything and everyone that directly brings more clients and money into your business and delivers your service, including: associate coaches; sales activities; sales associates; and marketing activities etc.

Red Category: all activities, systems and people that support your service delivery, including: administration assistants; financial management; and digital software Human Resources etc.

Black Category: your profit/valuation drivers such as branding and positioning in the market, strategies, and energy work, including: joint ventures; new product development; and opening new channels to market etc. You typically cannot directly measure the impact of black activities and systems on your business. However, it is a crucial element of all businesses on an extraordinary growth trajectory.

Nic's advice is to ensure the ratio of red, blue and black activities is correct for your specific stage of growth. Focus on a good quality blue category; manage red for maximum efficiency; and do some black. As much as possible do what it takes to strengthen your blue category in your business first. In the coaching space, we are taught to outsource everything that is not in our zone of genius. This is true, however, this encourages many coaches to hire a lot of red people only to find themselves working for the salaries of their team members. The answer is in fact to hire more blue people. Set measurable systems and key performance indicators to ensure that each person on your team will be profitable. Also, look at using digital software that doesn't only allow you to market yourself efficiently online, but gives you a great insight about how each of your marketing activities performs. According to Nic, the most profitable teams are the teams of four – three blue, one red, with the main person of influence - you - engaging in some black activities.

Think about this when setting up and expanding the infrastructure of your business. It will not only save you lots of money and energy, but can bring additional revenue to your business much faster. And of course, don't stop with people when offloading your To Do List. How about giving the big universe a few jobs to do too? In Chapter 9, I briefly described Mike Dooley's style of goal setting. You can use this whenever you feel a sense of overwhelm. Let the universe help you, which it will. Lastly, whenever you feel overwhelmed, the best thing you can do for yourself is to physically slow down. Take a few days off, no matter how impossible it may seem. Do something for fun, whatever will encourage you to embody the energy of the business you seek to build.

You see, when you slow down, you energetically speed up. You take your focus off the problems, off the tasks and away from the overwhelm and your resistance. Secondly, by consciously slowing down, you will choose time space. Time, as we talked about before, is a mind concept and it is flexible. When you consciously choose to create time space, you will more and more notice that you have more than enough time for everything. The following mantra might be a great one for you to practise when you are feeling under time pressure.

> *'The universe doesn't know such a thing as hurry or lack of time, because it can create things in no time'.*

4. Challenges: a sign that you are on your way to your greatest success

Unexpected bills; family dramas; temporary decrease in your revenues; and broken equipment. These are examples of challenges you may meet with when you set an intention for the next level of your business growth. Most women consider challenges a sign that what they aim for is unrealistic. They often use them as an excuse to give up or start again. However, you are not most women. You are an extraordinary woman and each and every challenge is a sign that you are closer than ever to your greatest success. You see, they happen because of one of the following three reasons:

1. De-selection: When you upgrade your consciousness and change your personal energy, that which isn't a match to you will naturally de-select itself. For some people, this may mean that potential clients who resonated with your marketing before will not resonate anymore. A few clients may cancel, others, while previously being a perfect match, will stop feeling that way. The same thing can also happen with suppliers, team members and even technology, such as computers breaking down and old equipment crashing on you. While this can surprise many people, it is a natural process and when that happens, you can be assured that you are incredibly closed to breaking through to your next, exciting level of business. Breakdown before breakthrough!

2. Echo of the old: When you start applying your personal energy differently, and—in layperson's language—vibe differently, you might still experience old circumstances for a little while. This is the echo of the old vibration and it means it is well and truly on its way out.

3. Opportunity for change: As we have already established, extraordinary growth requires extraordinary change on your part. The thing is, it is impossible to measure the change based on new, desired circumstances. You can measure how you have changed—or give yourself an opportunity for change—only by exposing yourself to undesired circumstance. For example, if you set an intention for more sales revenue and more abundance flowing into your experience, you might get an unexpected bill. How will you react to it? Will you react to it in an old way, getting worried? Or in a new way, in alignment with your higher mind, knowing that spending that money will bring ten times or more money back to you?

When dealing with challenges during your bridging period, remind yourself of one of Darryl Anka's powerful mantras: 'My circumstances do not matter. Only my state of being matters.' There is a deep meaning to this mantra and when you contemplate it, it can help you through times of trial, you know, when you are doing all the right things yet nothing is happening, as well as speeding up the process of the manifestation! Let's break it down. Circumstances do not matter. This means the obvious, that what you are experiencing right now doesn't matter much because any circumstance can change in an instant.

Ten minutes from now everything can be different. It really can. If you don't believe me, write down a list of experiences when things suddenly changed. But it also means that circumstances do not create. Circumstances never turn energy into matter. Only your state of being creates. Your state of being is your personal energy; a collection of thoughts, feelings and expectations. It is how you evaluate things; how you feel about them; and what you expect next. So, when you experience challenge on your way to extraordinary growth, remind yourself, 'My circumstances do not matter, only my state of being matters' and choose how you want to view the challenge.

Energetically speaking, there is no challenge that is intrinsically difficult. It is our evaluations of that challenge that make it so. This may sound crazy, or even insensitive to some, but unless death or health is involved, you will seek to evaluate your challenges differently. How about you see every challenge as fun and an incredible opportunity to grow in a big way? This alone can speed up bridging in a big way and help you remain in the Through Me Consciousness—the flow—while growing yourself and your business with it big time. You see, most people think of flow as a calm and steady river. Rapids, however, are also a form of flow, an inevitable part of up-scaling. When we fight it, we struggle; when we go with it and adjust accordingly, we experience accelerated change and growth.

Your destination is inevitable

My dear reader, we have arrived at the end of this book. You are now equipped with plenty of new perspectives, tools and ideas to help you to increase your sales; experience quantum leaps in your business; and set yourself on a never-ending journey of extraordinary growth. You are here, so the growth and miracles you would like to see in your business and life is yours. Inevitably.

But it needs to be said that this work is not the work of one afternoon. Extraordinary growth is not something you can compartmentalise into one hour a day. It is a lifestyle. It is a chosen state of being. Choose it daily, my gorgeous. Choose extraordinary growth. Choose yourself, because when you do, there are no limits to what kind of impact you can create in the world, and your life with it.

Use the following Extraordinary Growth Manifesto to be who you truly are: extraordinary.

With all my love

Lenka

THE EXTRAORDINARY WOMAN'S
BUSINESS GROWTH MANIFESTO

- ❦ We refuse to settle.
- ❦ We are willing to go through the discomfort of change.
- ❦ We are willing to bet on ourselves again and again, and choose growth rather than comfort.
- ❦ We are committed to serve and live at our highest level.
- ❦ We know what we stand for.
- ❦ There is no guesswork, we proudly share our message and adjust it as we grow.
- ❦ We know that what we want is here and now.
- ❦ Each day, we allow ourselves to accept what we want, more and more.
- ❦ We work daily on ourselves and on the way we relate to our internal power, clients, other people, selling, marketing and money.
- ❦ We know that our businesses are a reflection of our personal energy and can grow only as much as we do.
- ❦ We don't grow our businesses only through doing.
- ❦ We know that practicing new ways of being will take our businesses to greater heights than doing ever could.
- ❦ We learn and we learn all the time. We never hear the phrase, 'I know enough, I simply need to apply what I learned' from an extraordinary woman entrepreneur.

- ❦ We spend money to make money.
- ❦ We know that our business is not a piggy bank and it needs to eat to flourish.
- ❦ We make investments in our businesses and in ourselves in proportion to how fast and how much we want to grow.
- ❦ We stretch our trust muscles often.
- ❦ We don't always know the full 'how' with our physical minds.
- ❦ What we know, however, is that our higher-self is guiding us every step of the way, through our intuition.
- ❦ As we lean into trust more and more, we become more and more limitless.
- ❦ We don't always get it right and that is okay.
- ❦ We are willing to fail, more than once.
- ❦ We embrace failure, and do things better next time.
- ❦ We go deep instead of wide.
- ❦ We don't get caught up in the 'next shiny object' syndrome. Instead, we become aware of the skills and areas of business we need to master, and we work on them until we do so.
- ❦ We love to serve, and therefore we love to sell.
- ❦ We sell often, with passion and with certainty.
- ❦ We love our clients more than our fears.
- ❦ We never save our clients. We empower them.
- ❦ We dream bigger than anyone else we know, and we connect with our crazy big dreams often.
- ❦ We know that what we desire is the universe showing us how it wants to express itself through us and we honour it.
- ❦ Sometimes we are totally scared; and when we are, we negotiate with our ego and we do that thing that scares us anyway because we know that every time we do, we unlock the next level of growth.

- ❧ We cry when needed, we shout when needed, but we never give up.
- ❧ We know there is tremendous power in asking and we ask often.
- ❧ We celebrate ourselves, often.
- ❧ We never compare ourselves to other women entrepreneurs, only to our own yesterday.
- ❧ We stay focused on our growth; our clients; and our impact.
- ❧ We are in full control of money.
- ❧ We feel good about making loads of money by doing what we love because we know that the more money we make, the more difference we can make.
- ❧ We consciously take good care of ourselves.
- ❧ Even if it is not in our nature, we acknowledge that the more value we put on ourselves, the more value the world places on us.
- ❧ We take breaks, but we never stop.
- ❧ We never take anything as final.
- ❧ With each intention achieved, there is the next one.
- ❧ With each level of the business created, there is more growth to create.
- ❧ We don't believe in comfort zones.
- ❧ We ask for what we need.
- ❧ We consciously put ourselves even before our children and family members, because we know that is the only way to be able to truly give.
- ❧ We love giving, and we give a lot.
- ❧ We love receiving and we allow ourselves to receive, often.
- ❧ We are women of inspired action.
- ❧ We don't rely on the big universe to drop everything in our laps, for we know that our job is to create conditions for everything we want and we do that by doing the do.

- ✿ We stay detached from the outcomes of our actions, no matter how tricky at times.
- ✿ We know that as long as we are moving in alignment with our intentions, we are moving forward in the most perfect way.
- ✿ We love both business growth strategy and inner work. They are inseparable, and we aim to master both in harmony.
- ✿ We love this journey.
- ✿ We love entrepreneurship; with all its ups and downs, with all the good and the ugly, we would never change it for anything else.
- ✿ Even when our ego mind tells us otherwise at times, we know that we are destined to create a huge impact in the world and our own lives with it.
- ✿ Everything we experience is a gift, moving us towards our true destiny.
- ✿ We are extraordinary!

TAKE YOUR ENERGETIC SELLING & MARKETING MASTERY TO THE NEXT LEVEL!

Over the years, Lenka created a wealth of free and paid training resources that help women around the world to get fully booked with their ideal, high-end clients and scale their business to multiple six figures and beyond. Here are the two ways how you can benefit from them.

1. Free book resources

Visit **energeticselling.com/resources** to get your hands on the audio version of Activation Meditation, Energetic Selling Mastery Affirmations audio, and other training resources that will support you in your success.

2. Join Extraordinary Growth Academy

Extraordinary Growth Academy is Lenka's signature group coaching programme for women in business who desire to create extraordinary growth in their business. As a member of Extraordinary Growth Academy, you will get access to over £10,000 worth training courses with a customised study path; engaged and supportive online community of women entrepreneurs; regular group coaching sessions with Lenka and a lot more. Simply put, Extraordinary Growth Academy will give you everything you need to fulfil your potential as extraordinary woman entrepreneur.

Visit **lenkalutonska.com/ega-special** to learn more and claim 50% off regular membership fees.

3. Apply to talk to Lenka

Lenka takes on a select number of 1-2-1 and VIP Mastermind coaching clients each year. Should you like to explore working with Lenka privately, apply for a conversation with her by visiting **lenkalutonska.com/time-with-lenka**.

CHAPTER REFERENCES

Introduction
UG Krishnamurti – Indian speaker who questioned the state of enlightenment. Although many considered him an enlightened person, Krishnamurti often referred to his state of being as the natural state.

Chapter 1
Albert Einstein – German born theoretical physicist who developed the theory of relativity, one of the two pillars of modern physics alongside quantum mechanics.
Peter Sage – British serial international entrepreneur, expert in human behaviour, author *The Inside Track, 5 Keys To Master Your Life*, philosopher, speaker, coach and teacher.
Mihaly Csikszentmihalyi – Hungarian American psychologist who recognised and named the psychological concept of flow, as a highly focused mental state.

Chapter 2
Warren Buffet – American business magnate, investor, speaker and philanthropist.
Dr Jagdish Parikh – Indian international business mogul, consultant, speaker and author of *Managing Your Self: Management by Detached Involvement, Managing Relationships,* and *Making a Life While Making a Living.*
Thomas Edison – American inventor and businessman, credited with developing many devices in fields such as electric power generation, mass communication, sound recording and motion pictures.

228

Chapter References

Chapter 3

Alan Deutschman – American journalist, professor, author of *Change or Die; The Second Coming of Steve Jobs; A Tale of Two Valleys; Walk the Walk; How Steve Jobs Changed Our World.*

Chapter 4

Napoleon Hill – American self-help author of *Think and Grow Rich.*

Marianne Williamson – American spiritual teacher, author, lecturer, entrepreneur and activist. She has published 12 books, including four New York Times number one bestsellers. *A Return to Love* is considered a must-read for The New Spirituality.

Dr Joe Dispenza – American scientist, teacher, international speaker, researcher, corporate consultant and author of *You Are the Placebo: Making Your Mind Matter, Breaking the Habit of Being Yourself: How to Lose Your Mind and Create a New One, Evolve Your Brain: The Science of Changing Your Mind,* and *Becoming Supernatural* .

Albert Einstein – German born theoretical physicist who developed the theory of relativity, one of the two pillars of modern physics alongside quantum mechanics.

Greg Braden – American author of New Age literature and internationally renowned as a pioneer in bridging science, spirualty and human potential. He has published 12 award winning books and is five-time New York Times best selling author. Best known for *The Divine Matrix* and *The Spontaneous Healing of Belief.*

John Hagelin –American leader of the Transcendental Meditation movement in the United States.

Hagelin JS – Orme-Johnson DW; Rainforth M; Cavanaugh K; Alexander CN; Shatkin SF; Davies JL; Hughs AO; Ross E, *authors of Effects of Group Practice of the Transcendental Meditation Programme on Preventing Violent Crime* in Washington, D.C.: Results of the National Demonstration Project, June--July 1993', D C Institute of Science, Technology and Public Policy Technical Report, Social Indicators Research.

Chapter 5

Marie Forleo – American life coach, motivational speaker, entrepreneur, mentor author of *Make Every Man Want You* and web television host of award winning Marie TV.

Kimra Luna – American online entrepreneur and branding strategist.

Rob Brown – British motivational business speaker, author of *How to Build Your Reputation* and international authority on networking and referrals.

Dr Kavetha Sun, MD – Harvard trained psychiatrist and couples therapist.

Chapter 8

Ali ibn abi Talib – early Islamic leader.

Buddha – monk, mendicant, and sage on whose teachings Buddhism was founded.

Schultz, Mike and Doerr, John E – authors of *Insight Selling: Surprising Research on What Sales Winners Do Differently*, Hoboken, New Jersey: John Wiley & Sons.

Chapter 9

The Richest Man in Babylon – by George Samuel Clason that dispenses financial advice through a collection of parables set in ancient Babylon.

Mike Dooley – New York bestselling author, entrepreneur in the philosophical New Thought movement and creator of the wildly popular, *Notes from the Universe* whose many acclaimed books include, *Life on Earth, Leveraging the Universe*, and *Infinite Possibilities*.

Sue Knight – British international consultant and author of NLP At Work, pioneering the use of NLP for people in business.

Peter Drucker – Austrian born American management consultant, educator, and author of *The Effective Executive* among many others. His writings have contributed to the philosophical and practical foundations of the modern business corporation.

Chapter 10

Picasso – Spanish painter, sculptor, printmaker, ceramicist, stage designer, poet and playwright.

Sarah Morgan – Law of Attraction coach and author of *Welcome to the Beginning of Everything You Want*, and *It's Time To Get Your Money Flow On*.

Chapter 11

Nic Rixon – United Kingdom entrepreneur, strategist and author of *Design Your Life*.

Mike Dooley – New York bestselling author, entrepreneur in the philosophical New Thought movement and creator of the wildly popular, *Notes from the Universe* whose many acclaimed books include, *Life on Earth, Leveraging the Universe,* and *Infinite Possibilities.*

Darryl Anka – renowned channeller who brings through the multi-dimensional being from the future, known as Bashar.